YOUR INVISIBLE
POWER

AND

ATTAINING
YOUR DESIRES

ORIGINAL CLASSIC EDITIONS

Atom-Smashing Power of Mind

Crystallizing Public Opinion

How to Attract Money

Narrative of the Life of Frederick Douglass

Self Mastery Through Conscious Autosuggestion

The Art of War

The Magic of Believing

The Master Key System

The Power of Your Subconscious Mind

The Prince

The Richest Man in Babylon

The Science of Getting Rich

The Secret of the Ages

Think and Grow Rich

Think Your Way to Wealth

Your Invisible Power

YOUR INVISIBLE POWER

AND

ATTAINING YOUR DESIRES

Genevieve Behrend

MEDIA

Published 2021 by Gildan Media LLC
aka G&D Media
www.GandDmedia.com

YOUR INVISIBLE POWER AND ATTAINING YOUR DESIRES. Copyright © 2021
by G&D Media. Copyright 1921, 1927 by Genevieve Behrend. After-
word copyright © 2021 by Joe Vitale. All rights reserved.

Front cover design by David Rheinhardt of Pyrographx

Interior design by Meghan Day Healey of Story Horse, LLC

Library of Congress Cataloging-in-Publication Data is available upon
request

ISBN: 978-1-7225-0529-5

10   9   8   7   6   5   4   3   2   1

CONTENTS

YOUR
INVISIBLE
POWER

CONTENTS

INTRODUCTION

Genevieve Behrend was the only personal pupil that the great Thomas Troward ever had. She studied with him privately, at his home at Ruan Manor, Cornwall, England, for two years, 1912 to 1914, inclusive. She founded The School of the Builders in New York City and was the head of it until 1925. For five years thereafter she conducted the same school in Los Angeles and then toured the entire United States and Canada, presenting the Troward philosophy at its best, as only she was fully qualified to do, in almost every city of appreciable size.

She spent 35 years as one of America's greatest and best-known lecturers, teachers and practitioners. Millions heard and enjoyed her, not only on the public platform but over radio. Her students numbered tens of thousands all over the English-speaking world. Paris, France was her native city but she was half Scotch. This little book, *Your Invisible Power*, was her first. However it remains the most popular of all her books and has been, since its first edition, one of the world's best sellers on Mental Science. It has exhausted scores of editions.

Herein, Genevieve Behrend presents the Troward philosophy at its best, in her incomparable simple, direct and dynamic manner so well known to so many. Although she has written several other books this one remains her masterpiece.

—WORTH SMITH

Publisher's Note: Worth Smith, prominent author and authority on the Great Pyramid, has been the husband and closest collaborator of Genevieve Behrend for twenty-two years.

FOREWORD

These pages have been written for the purpose of furnishing you a key to the attainment of your desires, and to explain that Fear should be entirely banished from your consciousness in order for you to obtain possession of the things you want.

This pre-supposes, of course, that your desire for possession is based upon your aspiration for greater happiness. For example, you feel that the possession of more money, lands, or friends will make you happier, and your desire for possession of these things arises from a conviction that their possession will bring you freedom and contentment. In your effort to possess, you will discover that the thing you most need is to consistently "Be" your best self.

One morning after class a man came to me and asked if I would speak the word of supply for him, as he was sadly in the need of money. He offered me a $5 bill with the remark: "Dear Madam, that is half of every dollar I have in the world. I am in debt; my wife and child have not the proper clothing; in fact, I must have money." I explained to him that money was the symbol of differentiated substance, that this substance filled all space, that it was present for him at that very moment, and would manifest to him as the money he required. "But," he questioned, "it may come too late." I told him it could not come too late, as it was eternally present. He understood and got the uplift of my spoken word.

I did not see the man again, but six months later I had a letter from him stating he was in New Orleans. He said, "I am well established here in my regular profession of photography; I own my own home, have an automobile of my own, and am generally prospering. And dear Mrs. Behrend, I want to thank you for lifting me out of the depths that day in New York.

Three days after I talked to you, a man whom I have not seen for years met me on the street. When I explained my situation to him, be loaned me the money to pay my bills and come down here. The enclosed check is to help you continue your wonderful work of teaching people how to mentally reach out and receive their never-failing supply. I would not take anything for my understanding as you have given it to me. God bless you."

A feeling that greater possessions, no matter of what kind they may be, will of *themselves* bring contentment or happiness, is a misunderstanding. No person, place, or thing can give you happiness. They may give you cause for happiness and a feeling of contentment, but the Joy of Living comes from within.

Therefore, it is here recommended that you should make the effort to obtain the things which you feel will bring you joy, provided that your desires are in accord with the Joy of Living.

It is also desired, in this volume, to suggest the possibilities in store for all who make persistent effort to understand the Law of Visualization, and who make practical application of this knowledge on whatever plane they may be. The word "effort," as here employed, is not intended to convey the idea of strain. All study and meditation should be without strain or tension.

It has been my endeavor to show that by starting at the beginning of the creative action, or mental picture, certain corresponding results are sure to follow. "While the laws of the Universe cannot be altered, they can be made to work under specific conditions, thereby producing results for individual advancement which cannot be obtained under the spontaneous workings of the law provided by Nature."

However far these suggestions I have given—of the possibilities in store for you, through visualizing, may carry you beyond your past experience, they nowhere break the continuity of the law of cause and effect.

If through the suggestions here given, any one is brought to realize that his mind is a center through and in which "all power there is" is in operation, simply waiting to be given direction in the one and only way through which it can take specific action—and this means reaction in concrete or physical form—then the mission to which this book is dedicated has been fulfilled.

Try to remember that the picture you think, feel, and see is reflected into the Universal Mind, and by the natural law of reciprocal action must return to you in either spiritual or physical form. Knowledge of this law of reciprocal action between the individual and the Universal Mind opens to you free access to all you may wish to *possess* or to *be*.

It must be steadfastly borne in mind that all this can be true only for the individual who recognizes that he derives his power to make an abiding mental picture from the All-Originating Universal Spirit of Life, and can be used constructively only so long as it is employed and retained in harmony with the nature of the Spirit which originated it. To insure this there must be no inversion of the thought of the individual regarding his relationship to this Universal Originating Spirit, which is that of a son, through which the parent mind acts and reacts.

Thus conditioned, whatever you think and feel yourself to be, the Creative Spirit of Life is bound to faithfully reproduce in a corresponding reaction. This is the great reason for picturing yourself and your affairs the way you wish them to be as existing facts—though invisible to the physical eye—and living in your picture. An honest endeavor to do this, always recognizing that your own mind is a projection of the Originating Spirit, will prove to you that the best there is, is yours in all your ways.

—G.B.

Los Angeles, California;
May, 1929.

CHAPTER ONE

Order of Visualization

The exercise of the visualizing faculty keeps your mind in order, and attracts to you the things you need to make life more enjoyable in an orderly way.

If you train yourself in the practice of deliberately picturing your desire and carefully examining your picture, you will soon find that your thoughts and desires proceed in a more orderly procession than ever before.

Having reached a state of ordered mentality, you are no longer in a constant state of mental hurry. Hurry is Fear, and consequently destructive.

In other words, when your understanding grasps the power to visualize your heart's desire and hold it with your will, it attracts to you all things requisite to the fulfillment of that picture by the harmonious vibrations of the law of attraction.

You realize that since Order is Heaven's first law, and visualization places things in their natural order, then it must be a heavenly thing to visualize.

Everyone visualizes, whether he knows it or not. Visualizing is the great secret of success.

The conscious use of this great power attracts to you multiplied resources, intensifies your wisdom, and enables you to make use of advantages which you formerly failed to recognize.

A lady once came to me for help in selling a piece of property. After I explained to her just how to make a mental picture of the sale, going through the details mentally, exactly as she would do if the property were sold, she came a week later and told me how one day she was walking along the street, when the thought suddenly occurred to her to go and see a certain real estate dealer, to whom she had not yet been.

She hesitated for a moment when she first got the idea, as it seemed to her that that man could not sell her property. However, upon the strength of what I had told her, she followed the lead and went to the real estate man, who sold the property for her in just three days after she had first approached him. This was simply following along with the natural law of demand and supply.

We now fly through the air, not because anyone has been able to change the laws of Nature, but because the inventor of the flying machine learned how to apply Nature's laws and, by making orderly use of them, produced the desired result. So far as the natural forces are concerned, nothing has changed since the beginning. There were no airplanes in "the Year One," because those of that generation could not conceive the idea as a practical, working possibility. "It has not yet been done," was the argument, "and it cannot be done." Yet the laws and materials for practical flying machines existed then as now.

Troward tells us that the great lesson he learned from the airplane and wireless telegraphy is the triumph of principle over precedent, the working out of an idea to its logical conclusion in spite of accumulated contrary testimony of all past experience.

With such an example before you, you must realize that there are still greater secrets to be disclosed. Also, "That you hold the key within yourself, with which to unlock the secret chamber that contains your heart's desire.

All that is necessary in order that you may use this key and make your life exactly what you wish it to be, is a careful inquiry into the unseen causes which stand back of every external and visible condition. Then bring these unseen causes into harmony with your conception, and you will find that you can make practical working realities of possibilities which at present seem but fantastic dreams."

A woman came to me in New York City, asking for help, as she was out of work. I spoke the word of ever-present supply for her and intensified it by mentally seeing the woman in the position she dreamed of, but which she had been unable to make a practical reality.

That same afternoon she telephoned and said she could hardly believe her senses, as she had just taken exactly the kind of a position she wanted. The employer told her she had been wanting a woman like her for months.

We all knew that the balloon was the forefather of the airplane. In 1766 Henry Cavendish, an English nobleman, proved that hydrogen gas was seven times lighter than air. From that discovery the balloon came into existence, and from the ordinary balloon the dirigible, a cigar-shaped airship, was evolved.

Study of aeronautics and laws of the aerial locomotion of birds and projectiles led to the belief that mechanism could be evolved by which heavier-than-air machines could be made to travel from place to place and remain in the air by the maintenance of great speed, which would overcome by propulsive force the ordinary law of gravitation. Professor Langley of Washington, who developed much of the theory which others afterward improved upon, was subjected to much derision when he sent a model airplane up, only to have it bury its nose in the muddy waters of the Potomac. But the Wright Brothers, who experimented later, realized the possibility of traveling through the air in a machine that had no gas bag. They *saw* themselves enjoying this mode of transportation with great facility. It is said that one of the brothers would tell the other, when their varied experiences did not turn out as they expected:

"It's all right, Brother, I can *see* myself riding in that machine, and it travels easily and steadily."

Those Wright Brothers knew what they wanted and kept their pictures constantly before them. Now transportation through the air is developing rapidly and we all feel sure it will in the near future become as ordinary a method of travel as the automobile.

In visualizing, or making a mental picture, you are not endeavoring to change the laws of Nature. You are fulfilling them.

Your object in visualizing is to bring things into regular order, both mentally and physically. When you realize that this method of employing the Creative Power brings your desires, one after another, into practical, material accomplishment, your confidence in the mysterious but unfailing law of attraction, which has its central power station in the very heart of your word-picture, becomes supreme. Nothing can shake it. You never feel that it is necessary to take anything from anybody else. You have learned that asking and seeking have, as their correlatives, receiving and finding. You know that all you have to do is to start the plastic substance of the Universe flowing into the thought-molds your picture-desire provides.

CHAPTER TWO

How to Attract to Yourself the Things You Desire

The power within you which enables you to form a thought-picture is the starting point of all there is. In its original state it is the undifferentiated formless substance of life. Your thought-picture makes the model, so to say, into which this formless substance takes shape.

Visualizing, or mentally seeing things and conditions as you wish the to be, is the condensing, the specializing power in you which might be illustrated by comparison with the lens of a magic lantern, which is one of the best symbols of the imaging faculty.

It illustrates the idea of the working of the Creative Spirit on the plane of initiative and selection—or in its concentrated, specializing form—in a remarkably clear manner.

The picture slide illustrates your own mental picture—invisible in the lantern of your mind until you turn on the light of your will.

That is to say, you light up your desire with absolute faith that the Creative Spirit of Life, in you, is doing the work. By the steady flow of the light of the Will on the Spirit, your desired picture is projected upon the screen of the physical world—an exact reproduction of the pictured slide in your mind.

A woman came to me for help to cause her husband to return to her. She said she was very unhappy and lonely without him and longed to be reunited. I told her she could not lose love and protection, because both belonged to her. She asked what she should do to get her husband back again. I told her to follow the great power of intuition and think of her husband as perfectly free, and the embodiment of all that a husband should be.

She went away quite happy, but returned in a few days to tell me that her husband desired a divorce in order to marry again. She was quite agitated and had evidently relaxed her will in following the instructions given at the former interview. Again I told her to hold constantly in her mind that the loving protection of the Spirit of Life would guide her in perfect happiness.

A month later she came again and said that her husband had married the other woman. This time she had completely lost her mental grip. I repeated the words for her as before, and she regained her poise. Two months later she came back to me, full of joy. Her husband had come to her, begging her forgiveness, and telling her what a terrible mistake he had made, as he could not be happy without her. They are now living happily together, and she, at least, learned the necessity of holding her pictured desire steadily in place by the use of her will.

Visualizing without a will sufficiently steady to inhibit every thought and feeling contrary to your pictured thought would be as useless as a magic lantern without the light.

On the other band, if your will is sufficiently developed to bold your picture in thought and feeling, without any "ifs"; simply realizing that your thought is the great attracting power, then your mental picture is as certain to be projected upon your physical world as a picture slide put into a magic lantern shows on the screen.

Try projecting the picture in a magic lantern with a light that is constantly shifting from one side to the other, and you will produce the effect of an uncertain will. It is as necessary that you should always have back of your picture a strong, steady will, as it is to have a strong steady light back of a picture slide.

The joyous assurance with which you make your picture is the very powerful magnet of Faith, and nothing can obliterate it. You are happier than you ever were, because you have learned to know where your source of supply is, and you rely upon its never-failing response to the direction you give it.

All said and done, happiness is the one thing which every human being wants, and the study of visualization enables you to get more out of life than you ever enjoyed before. Increasing possibilities keep opening out, more and more, before you.

A business man once told me that since practicing visualization, and forming the habit of devoting a few minutes each day to thinking about his work as he desired it to be, in a large, broad way, his orders had more than doubled in six months.

His method was to go into a room every morning before breakfast and take a mental inventory of his business as he had left it the evening before, and then enlarge upon it. He said he expanded and expanded in this way, until his affairs were in a remarkably successful condition. He would see himself in his office doing everything he wanted done. His occupation required him to meet many strangers every day.

In his mental picture he saw himself meeting these people, understanding their needs, and supplying them in just the way they wished. This habit, he said, had strengthened and steadied his will in an almost inconceivable manner.

Furthermore, by thus mentally seeing things as he wished them to be, he had acquired the confident feeling that a certain Creative Power was exercising itself, for him and through him, for the purpose of improving his little world.

When you first begin to visualize seriously, you may feel, as many others do, that someone else may be forming the same picture you are, and that, naturally, would not suit your purpose. Do not give yourself any concern about this.

Simply try to realize that your picture is an orderly exercise of the Universal Creative Power specifically applied. Then you may be sure that no one can work in opposition to you. The universal law of harmony prevents that.

Endeavor to bear in mind that your mental picture is Universal Mind specifically exercising its inherent powers of initiative and selection. God, or Universal Mind, made man for the special purpose of differentiating Himself through him. Everything there is, came into existence in this same way, by this self-same law of self-differentiation, and for the same purpose. First came the idea, the mental picture, or the prototype of the thing, which is the thing itself in its incipiency.

The Great Architect of the Universe contemplated Himself as manifesting through his polar opposite— matter—and the idea expanded and projected itself until we have not only a world, but many worlds.

Many people ask, "But why should we have a physical world at all ?" The answer is:

"Because it is the nature of Originating Substance to solidify, under directivity rather than activity, just as it is the nature of wax to harden when it becomes cold, or plaster of paris to become firm and solid when exposed to the air."

Your picture is this same Divine Substance in its original state, taking form through the individualized center of Divine operation, in your mind; and there is no power to prevent this combination of Spiritual Substance from becoming physical form. It is the nature of Spirit to complete its work, and an idea is not complete until it has made for itself a vehicle.

Nothing can prevent your picture from coming into concrete form except the same power which gave it birth—yourself.

Suppose you wish to have a more orderly room. You look about your room, and the idea of order suggests boxes, closets, shelves, hooks, and so forth. The box, the closet and the hooks, are all concrete ideas of order, because they are the vehicles through which order and harmony suggest themselves.

CHAPTER THREE

Relation Between Mental and Physical Form

Some persons feel that it is not quite proper to visualize for *things.* "It's too material," they say. Why, material form is necessary for the self-recognition of Spirit from the individual standpoint, and this is the means through which the Creative Process is carried forward.

Therefore, far from matter being an illusion and something which ought not to be, matter is the necessary channel for the self-differentiation of Spirit.

However, it is not my desire to lead you into lengthy and tiresome scientific reasoning, in order to remove the mystery from visualization and to put it upon a logical foundation.

Naturally, each individual will do this in his own way. My only wish is to point out to you the easiest way I know, which is the road on which Troward guides me. I feel sure you will conclude, as I have, that the only mystery in connection with visualizing is the mystery of life taking form, governed by unchangeable and easily understood laws.

We all possess more power and greater possibilities than we realize, and visualizing is one of the greatest of these powers, it brings other Possibilities to our observation. When we pause to think for a moment, we realize that for a cosmos to exist at all, it must be the outcome of a Cosmic Mind, which binds "all individual minds to a certain generic unity of action, thereby producing all things as realities and nothing as illusions." If you will take this thought of Troward's and meditate upon it without prejudice, you will surely realize that concrete material form is an absolute necessity of the Creative Process; also "that matter is not an illusion but a necessary channel thru which life differentiates itself." If you consider matter in its right order, as the polar opposite to Spirit, you will not find any antagonism between them. On the contrary, together they constitute one harmonious whole. And when you realize this, you feel, in your practice of visualizing, that you are working from cause to effect, from beginning to end. In reality your mental picture is the specialized outworking of the Originating Spirit. One could talk for hours on purely scientific lines, showing, as Troward says, "that raw material for the formation of the solar systems is universally distributed throughout all space. Yet investigation shows that while the Heavens are studded with millions of suns, there are spaces which show no signs of cosmic activity. This being true, There must be something which started cosmic activity in certain places, while passing over others in which the raw material was equally available. At first thought, one might attribute development of cosmic energy to the etheric particles themselves. Upon investigation however, we find that this is mathematically impossible in a medium which is equally distributed throughout space, for all its particles are in equilibrium; therefore, no one particle possesses in itself a greater power of originating motion than the other. Thus we find that the initial movement, though working in and through the particles of primary substance, is not the particles themselves. It is this something we mean when we speak of Spirit."

This same power that brought universal substance into existence will bring your individual thought or mental picture into physical form. There is no difference in the power. The only difference is a difference of degree. The power and the substance themselves are the same. Only in working out your mental picture, it has transferred its creative energy from the Universal to the particular, and is working in the same unfailing manner from its specific center, your mind.

CHAPTER FOUR

Operation of Your Mental Picture

The operation of a large telephone system may be used as a simile. The main, or head central subdivides itself into many branch centrals, every branch being in direct connection with the main central, and each individual branch recognizing the source of its existence, reports all things to its central head. Therefore, when assistance of any nature is required: new supplies, difficult repairs to be done, or what not, the branch in need goes at once to its central head. It would not think of referring its difficulties (or its successes) to the main central of a telegraph system, though they might belong to the same organization. These different

branch centrals know that the only remedy for any difficulty must come from the central out of which they
were projected and to which they are always attached.

If we, as individual branches of the Universal Mind,
would refer our difficulties in the same confident manner to the source from which we were projected, and
use the remedies which it has provided, we would realize what Jesus meant when he said, "Ask and ye shall
receive." Our every requirement would be met. Surely
the Father must supply the child. The trunk of the tree
cannot fail to provide for its branches.

A man came to me in great distress, saying he was
about to lose his home in the South. In his own words,
it was mortgaged to the hilt, and his creditors were
going to foreclose. It was the house in which he had
been born and had grown to young manhood, and the
thought of losing it filled his heart and mind with sorrow, not only from a money standpoint, but from the
standpoint of sentimental association. I explained to
him that the Power that brought him into existence
did so for the purpose of expressing its limitless supply
through him; that there was no power on earth which
could cut him off from his source except his own consciousness, and that in reality he would not be cut off
then. I explained to him that he had it, but was unable
to recognize that it was there, and said to him, "Infinite
substance is manifesting in you right now." The next
week, on Sunday, just before leaving my dressing room

in the Selwyn Theatre to give my afternoon message, I received the following note: "Dear Mrs. Behrend: I want you to know that I am the happiest man in the whole city of New York. My home in the South is saved. The money came in the most miraculous way, and I have telegraphed enough to pay off the mortgage. Please tell the people this afternoon about this wonderful Power."

You may be sure I did, explaining to them that everything animate or inanimate is called into existence or outstandingness by a Power which itself does not stand out. The Power which creates the mental picture—the Originating Spirit Substance of your pictured desire—does not stand out. It projects the substance of itself, which is a solidified counterpart of itself, while it—the Power—remains invisible to the physical eye. Those will appreciate the value of visualizing who are able to realize Paul's meaning when he said, "The worlds were formed by the word of God. Things which are seen are not made of things which do appear."

There is nothing unusual or mysterious in the idea of your pictured desire coming into material evidence. It is the working of a universal, natural Law. The world was projected by the self-contemplation of the Universal Mind, and this same action is taking place in its individualized branch which is the Mind of Man. Everything in the whole world, from the hat on your head to the boots on your feet, has its beginning in mind and comes into existence in exactly the same manner. All are projected thoughts, solidified. Your personal advance in evolution depends on your right use of the power of visualizing, and your use of it depends on whether you recognize that you, yourself, are a particular center through and in which the Originating Spirit is finding ever new expression for potentialities already existing within Itself. This is evolution.

Your mental picture is the force of attraction which evolves and combines the Originating Substance into specific shape. Your picture is the combining and evolving power house, in a generative sense, so to say, through which the Originating Creative Spirit expresses itself. Its creative action is limitless, without beginning and without end, and always progressive and orderly. "It proceeds stage by stage, each stage being a necessary preparation for the one to follow." Now let us see if we can get an idea of the different stages by which the things in the world have come to be. Troward says, "If we can get at the working principle which is producing these results, we can very quickly and easily give it personal application. First, we find that the thought of Originating Life, or Spirit, concerning Itself is its simple awareness of its own being, and this, demanding a relationship to something else, produces a primary ether, a universal substance out of which everything in the world must grow."

Troward also tells us that "though this awareness of being is a necessary foundation for any further possibilities, it is not much to talk about." It is the same with individualized Spirit, which is yourself. Before you can entertain the idea of making a mental picture of your desire as being at all practical, you must have some idea of your being; of your "I am"; and just as soon as you are conscious of your "I-amness," you begin to wish to enjoy the freedom which this consciousness suggests. You want to do more and be more, and as you fulfill this desire within yourself, localized spirit begins conscious activities in you. The thing you are more concerned with is the specific action of the Creative Spirit of Life, Universal Mind specialized. The localized God-germ in you is your personality, your individuality and since the joy of absolute freedom is the inherent nature of this God-germ, it is natural that it should endeavor to enjoy itself through its specific center. And as you grow in the comprehension that your being, your individuality, is God particularizing Himself, you naturally develop Divine tendencies. You want to enjoy life and liberty. You want freedom in your affairs as well as in your consciousness, and it is natural that you should. With this progressive wish there is always a faint thought-picture. As your wish and your recognition grow into an intense desire, this desire becomes a clear mental picture. For example, a young lady studying music wishes she had a piano in order to practice at home. She wants the piano so much that she can mentally see it in one of the rooms. She holds the picture of the piano and indulges in the mental reflection of the pleasure and advantage it will be to have the piano in the corner of the living room. One day she finds it there, just as she had pictured it.

As you grow in understanding as to who you are, where you came from, what the purpose of your being is, and how you are to fulfill the purpose for which you are intended, you will become a more and more perfect center through which the Creative Spirit of Life can enjoy itself. And you will realize that there can be but one creative process filling all space, which is the same in its potentiality whether universal or individual. Furthermore, all there is, whether on the plane of the visible or invisible, had its origin in the localized action of thought, or a mental picture, and this includes yourself, because you are Universal Spirit localized, and the same creative action is taking place through you.

Now you are no doubt asking yourself why there is so much sickness and misery in the world. If the same power and intelligence which brought the world into existence is in operation in the mind of man, why does it not manifest itself as strength joy, health and plenty? If one can have one's desires fulfilled by simply making a mental picture of that desire, holding on to it with the will, and without anxiety, doing on the outward plane whatever seems necessary to bring the desire into fulfillment, then there seems no reason for the existence of sickness and poverty. Surely no one desires either. The first reason is that few persons will take the trouble to inquire into the working principle of the Laws of Life. If they did, they would soon convince themselves that there is no necessity for the sickness and poverty which we see about us. They would realize that visualizing is a principle and not a fallacy. There are a few who have found it worth while to study this simple, though absolutely unfailing law, which will deliver them from bondage. However, the race as a whole is not willing to give the time required for the study. It is either too simple, or too difficult. They may make a picture of their desire with some little understanding of visualizing for a day or two, but more frequently it is for an hour or so.

If you will insist upon mentally seeing yourself surrounded by things and conditions as you wish them to be you will understand that the Creative Energy sends its substance in the direction indicated by the tendency of your thoughts. Herein lies the advantage of holding your thought in the form of a mental picture.

A man in the hardware business in New Jersey came to me in great distress. He would have to go into bankruptcy unless something happened in a fortnight.

He said he had never heard of visualizing. I explained to him how to make a mental picture of his business increasing, instead of a picture of losing it. In about a month's time he returned very happy and told me how he had succeeded. He said, "I have my debts all paid, and my shop is full of new supplies." His business was then on a solid basis. It was beautiful to see his Faith.

The more enthusiasm and faith you are able to put into your picture, the more quickly it will come into visible form, and your enthusiasm is increased by keeping your desire secret. The moment you speak it to any living soul, that moment your power is weakened. Your power, your magnet of attraction is not that strong, and consequently cannot reach so far. The more perfectly a secret between your mind and your outer self is guarded, the more vitality you give your power of attraction. One tells one's troubles to weaken them, to get them off one's mind, and when a thought is given out, its power is dissipated. Talk it over with yourself, and even write it down, then destroy the paper.

However, this does not mean that you should strenuously endeavor to compel the Power to work out your picture on the special lines that you think it should. That method would soon exhaust you and hinder the fulfillment of your purpose. A wealthy relative need not necessarily die, or someone lose a fortune on the street, to materialize the $10,000 which you are mentally picturing. One of the doormen in the building in which I lived heard much of the mental picturing of desires from visitors passing out of my rooms. The average desire was for $500. He considered that five dollars was more in his line and began to visualize it, without the slightest idea of where or how he was to get it. My parrot flew out of the window, and I telephoned to the men in the courtyard to get it for me. One caught it, and it bit him on the finger. The doorman, who had gloves on, and did not fear a similar hurt, took hold of it and brought it up to me. I gave him five one dollar bills for his service. This sudden reward surprised him. He enthusiastically told me that he had been visualizing for just $5, merely from hearing that others visualized. He was delighted at the unexpected realization of his mental picture.

All you have to do is to make such a mental picture of your heart's desire, and hold it cheerfully in place with your will, always conscious that the same Infinite Power which brought the universe into existence, brought you into form for the purpose of enjoying Itself in and through you. And since it is all Life, Love, Light, Power, Peace, Beauty, and Joy, and is the only Creative Power there is, the form it takes in and through you depends upon the direction given it by your thought. In you it is undifferentiated, waiting to take any direction given it as it passes through the instrument which it has made for the purpose of self-distribution—you.

It is this Power which enables you to transfer your thoughts from one form to another. The power to change your mind is the individualized Universal Power taking the initiative, giving direction to the unformed substance contained in every thought.

It is the simplest thing in the world to give this highly sensitive Substance any form you will, through visualizing. Anyone can do it with a small expenditure of effort. Once you really believe that your mind is a center through which the unformed substance of all there is in your world, takes involuntary form, the only reason your picture does not always materialize is because you have introduced something antagonistic to the fundamental principle. Very often this destructive element is caused by the frequency with which you change your pictures. After many such changes, you decide that your original desire is what you want after all. Upon this conclusion, you begin to wonder why it (being your first picture) has not materialized. The Substance with which you are mentally dealing is more sensitive than the most sensitive photographer's film. If, while taking a picture, you suddenly remembered you had already taken a picture on that same plate, you would not expect a perfect result of either picture. On the other hand, you may have taken two pictures on the same plate unconsciously. When the plate has been developed, and the picture comes into physical view, you do not condemn the principle of photography, nor are you puzzled to understand why your picture has turned out so unsatisfactorily. You do not feel that it is impossible for you to obtain a good, clear picture of the subject in question. You know that you can do so, by simply starting at the beginning, putting in a new plate, and determining to be more careful while taking your picture next time. If these lines are followed out, you are sure of a satisfactory result. If you will proceed in the same manner with your mental picture, doing your part in a correspondingly confident frame of mind, the result will be just as perfect. The laws of visualizing are as infallible as the laws governing photography. In fact, photography is the outcome of visualizing.

Again, your results in visualizing the fulfillment of your desires may be imperfect, and your desires delayed, through the misuse of this power, owing to the thought that the fulfillment of your desire is contingent upon certain persons or conditions. The Originating Principle is not in any way dependent upon any person, place, or thing. It has no past and knows no future. The law is that the Originating Creative Principle of Life is "the universal here and everlasting now." It creates its own vehicles through which to operate. Therefore, past experience has no bearing upon your present picture. So do not try to obtain your desire through a channel which may not be natural for it, even though it may seem reasonable to you. Your feeling should be that the thing, or the consciousness, which you so much desire, is normal and natural, a part of yourself, a form of your evolution. If you can do this, there is no power to prevent your enjoying the fulfillment of the picture you have in mind, or any other you may create.

CHAPTER FIVE

Expressions from Beginners

Hundreds of persons have realized that "visualizing is an Aladdin's lamp to him with a mighty will." General Foch says that his feelings were so outraged during the Franco-Prussian war in 1870 that he visualized himself leading a French army against the Germans to victory. He said he made his picture, smoked his pipe, and waited. This is one result of visualizing with which we are all familiar.

A famous actress wrote a long article in one of the leading Sunday papers last winter, describing how she rid herself of excessive avoirdupois by seeing her figure constantly as she wished to be.

A very interesting letter came to me from a doctor's wife, while I was lecturing in New York. She began with the hope that I would never discontinue my lectures on visualization, which were helping humanity to realize the wonderful fact that they possessed the means of liberation within themselves. Relating her own experience, she said that she was born on the East Side of New York in the poorest quarter. From earliest girlhood she had cherished a dream of marrying a physician some day. This dream gradually formed a stationary mental picture. The first position she obtained was in the capacity of a maid in a physician's family. Leaving this place, she entered the family of another doctor. The wife of her employer died, and in the doctor married her—the result of long-pictured yearning. After that, both and her husband conceived the idea of owning a fruit farm in the South. They formed a mental picture of the idea and put their faith in its eventual fulfillment. The letter she sent me came from her fruit farm in the South. Her second mental picture had seen the light of materialization.

Many letters of a similar nature come to me every day. The following is a case that was printed in the New York Herald last May:

"Atlantic City, May 5—She was an old woman, and when she was arraigned before Judge Clarence Goldenberg in the police court today she was so weak and tired she could hardly stand. The Judge asked the court attendant what she was charged with. 'Stealing a bottle of milk, Your Honor,' repeated the officer. 'She took it from the doorstep of a downtown cottage before daybreak this morning.' 'Why did you do that?' Judge Golden-berg asked her. 'I was hungry,' the old woman said. 'I didn't have a cent in the world and no way to get anything to eat except to steal it. I didn't think anybody would mind if I took a bottle of milk.' 'What's your name?' asked the judge. 'Weinberg,' said the old woman, 'Elizabeth Weinberg.' Judge Goldenberg asked her a few questions about herself. Then he said:

"'Well, you're not very wealthy now, but you're no longer poor. I've been searching for you for months. I've got $500 belonging to you from the estate of a relative. I am the executor of the estate.'

"Judge Goldenberg paid the woman's fine out of his own pocket, and then escorted her into his office, where he turned her legacy over to her and sent a policeman out to find her a lodging place."

I learned later that this little woman had been desiring and mentally picturing $500, while all the time ignorant of how it could possibly come to her. But she kept her vision and strengthened it with her faith.

In an issue of Good Housekeeping there was an article by Addington Bruce entitled "Stiffening Your Mental Backbone." It is very instructive, and would benefit anyone to read it. He says, in part: "Form the habit of devoting a few moments every day to thinking about your work in a large, broad, imaginative way, as a vital necessity to yourself and a useful service to society."

James J. Hill, the great railway magnate, before he started building his road from coast to coast, said that he took hundreds of trips all along the line before there was a rail laid. It is said that he would sit for hours with a map of the United States before him and mentally travel from coast to coast, just as we do now over his fulfilled mental picture. It would be possible to call your attention to hundreds of similar cases.

The method of picturing to yourself what you desire is both simple and enjoyable, if you once understand the principle back of it well enough to believe it. Over and above everything else, be sure of what it is you really want. Then specialize your desire along the lines given in the following chapter.

CHAPTER SIX

Suggestions for Making Your Mental Picture

Perhaps you want to feel that you've lived to some purpose. You want to be contented and happy; you feel that good health and a successful business would give you contentment. After you have decided once and for all that this is what you want, you proceed to picture yourself healthy, and your business just as great a success as you can naturally conceive it growing into. The best times for making your definite picture are just before breakfast, and again, before retiring at night. As it is necessary to give yourself plenty of time,it may be necessary to rise earlier than you usually do. Go into a room where you will not be disturbed, meditate for a few moments upon the practical working of the law of visualizing, and ask yourself, "How did the things about me first come into existence? How can I get more quickly in touch with my invisible supply?"

Someone felt that comfort would be better expressed and experienced by sitting on a chair than on the floor. So the very beginning of a chair was the desire to be at ease. With this came the picture of some sort of a chair, The same principle applies to the hat and the clothes you wear. Go carefully into the thought of the principle back of the thing. Establish it as a personal experience; make it a fact to your consciousness. Then open a window, take about ten deep breaths, and during the time draw a large imaginary circle of light pound you. As you inhale—keeping yourself in the center of this circle of light—see great rays of light coming from the circle and entering your body at all points, centralizing itself at your solar plexus. Hold the breath a few moments at this central point of your body—the solar plexus—then slowly exhale. As you do this, mentally see imaginary rays, or sprays, of light going up through the body, and down and out through feet. Mentally spray your entire body with this imaginary light. When you have finished the breathing exercise, sit in a comfortable upright chair and mentally know there is but one Life, one Substance, and this Life Substance of the Universe is finding pleasure in self-recognition in you. Repeat some affirmation of this kind, until you feel the truth and stimulating reality of the words which you are affirming. Then begin your picture. If you are thorough in this, you will find yourself in the deep consciousness beneath the surface of your own thought power.

Whether your desire is for a state of consciousness, or a possession, large or small, begin at the beginning. If you want a house, begin by seeing yourself in the kind of house you desire. Go all through it, taking careful note of the rooms, where the windows are situated, and such other details as help you to feel the reality of your picture. You might change some of the furniture about and look into some of the mirrors just to see how healthy, wealthy, and happy you look. Go over your picture again and again, until you feel the reality of it, then write it all down just as you have seen it, with the feeling that:

"The best there is, is mine. There is no limit to me, because my mind is a center of divine operation," and your picture is as certain to come true, in your physical world, as the sun is to shine.

CHAPTER SEVEN

*Things to Remember
in Using Your Thought
Power for the Production
of New Conditions*

In Using Your Thought Power for the Production of New Conditions

1. Be sure to know exactly what conditions wish to produce. Then weigh carefully what further results the accomplishment of your desire will lead to.

2. By letting your thought dwell upon a mental picture, you are concentrating the Creative Action of Spirit in this center, where its forces are equally balanced.

3. Visualizing brings your objective mind into a state of equilibrium, which enables you to consciously direct the flow of Spirit to a definitely recognized purpose, and to carefully guard your thoughts from including a flow in the opposite direction.

4. You must always bear in mind that you are dealing with a wonderful potential energy, which is not yet differentiated into any particular form, and that by the action of your mind, you can differentiate it into any specific form that you will. Your picture assists you to keep your mind fixed on the fact that the inflow of this Creative Energy is taking place. Also, by your mental picture, you are determining the direction you wish the sensitive Creative Power to take, and by doing this, you make the externalization of your picture a certainty.

5. Remember when you are visualizing properly that there is no strenuous effort to hold your thought-forms in place. Strenuous effort defeats your purpose, and suggests the consciousness of an adverse force to be fought against, and this creates conditions adverse to your picture.

6. By holding your picture in a cheerful frame of mind, you shut out all thoughts that would disperse or dissipate the spiritual nucleus of your picture.

Because the law is Creative in its action, your pictured desire is certain of accomplishment.

7. The seventh and great thing to remember in visualizing is that you are making a mental picture for the purpose of determining the quality you are giving to the previously undifferentiated substance and energy, rather than to arrange the specific circumstances for its manifestation. That is the work of Creative Power itself. It will build its own forms of expression quite naturally, if you will allow it, and save you a great deal of needless anxiety. What you really want is expansion in a certain direction, whether of health, wealth, or what not, and so long as you get it—as you surely will, if you confidently hold to your picture—what does it matter whether it reaches by some channel which you thought you could count upon, or through some other of whose existence you had no idea. You are concentrating energy of a particular kind for a particular purpose. Keep this in mind and let specific details take care of themselves, and never mention what you are doing to anyone.

Remember always, that "Nature, from her clearly visible surface to her most arcane depths, is one vast storehouse of light and good entirely devoted to your individual use." Your conscious Oneness with the great Whole is the secret of success, and when once you have fathomed this, you can enjoy your possession of the whole, or a part of it, at will, because by your recognition you have made it, and can increasingly make it, yours.

Never forget that every physical thing, whether for you or against you, was a sustained thought before it was a thing. Thought, as thought, is neither good nor bad; it is Creative Action and always takes physical form. Therefore, the thoughts you dwell upon become the things you possess or do not possess.

A man came to me telling me how be longed to marry a certain young woman, but felt he could not afford to as his salary was small, and work uncertain. I spoke the word of ever-present Certain, Unlimited Supply and explained that Love knows no failure.

"It is yours to enjoy. See yourself in the kind of a home you both want. Do your part, keep on loving the girl, and believe absolutely in that which Lives and Loves in you."

A few months later they both came to my study looking radiantly happy. I knew they were married. The wife said to me: "Dear Mrs. Behrend, we are very happy because we now know how to use our thought power and hold our consciousness as one, with all we want."

So be yourself and enjoy Life in your own Divine way. Do not fear to be your true self, for everything you want, wants you.

CHAPTER EIGHT

Why I Took Up the Study of Mental Science

I have frequently been questioned about my reasons for taking up the study of Mental Science, and as to the results of my search, not only in the knowledge of principles, but also in the application of that knowledge for the development of my own life.

Such inquiries are justifiable, because one who essays the role of a messenger of psychological truths can only be convincing as he or she has tested them in the laboratory of personal mental experience. This is particularly true in my case, as the only personal pupil of Judge Troward, the great Master in Mental Science, whose teaching is based upon the relation borne by the Individual Mind toward the Universal Creative Mind, which is the Giver of Life, and the manner in which that relation may be invoked to secure expansion and fuller expression in the individual life.

My initial impulse toward the study of Mental Science was an overwhelming sense of loneliness. In every life there must come some such experience of spiritual isolation as pervaded my life at that period. Notwithstanding the fact that each day found me in the midst of friends, surrounded by mirth and gaiety, there was a persistent feeling that I was alone in the world. I had been a widow for about three years, wandering from country to country, seeking for peace of mind.

The circumstances and surroundings of my life were such that my friends looked upon me as an unusually fortunate young woman. Although they recognized that I had sustained a great loss when my husband died, they knew that he had left me well provided for, free to go anywhere my pleasure dictated.

Yet, if my friends could have penetrated my inmost emotions, they would have found a deep sense of emptiness and isolation. This feeling inspired a spirit of unrest, which drove me on and on in fruitless search upon the outside, for that which I later learned could only be found within.

I studied Christian Science, but it gave me no solace, though fully realizing the, great work the Scientists were doing, and even having the pleasure and privilege of meeting Mrs. Eddy personally. But it was impossible for me to accept the fundamental teachings of Christian Science and make practical application of it.

When about to abandon the search for contentment and resign myself to resume a life of apparent amusement, a friend invited me to visit the great Seer and Teacher, Abdul Baha. After my interview with this most wonderful of men, my search for contentment began to take a change. He had told me that I would travel the world over seeking the truth, and when I had found it, would speak it out. The fulfillment of the statement of this Great Seer then seemed to be impossible. But it carried a measure of encouragement, and at least indicated that my former seeking had been in the wrong direction. I began in a feeble groping way to find contentment within myself, for had he not intimated that I should find the truth? That was the big thing, and about the only thing I remember of our interview.

A few days later, upon visiting the office of a New Thought practitioner, my attention was attracted to a book on his table entitled *The Edinburgh Lectures on Mental Science*, by T. Troward. It interested me to see that Troward was a retired Divisional Judge from the Punjab, India. I purchased the book, thinking I would read it through that evening. Many have endeavored to do the same thing, only to find, as I did, that the book must be studied in order to be understood, and hundreds have decided, just as I did, to give it their undivided attention. After finding this treasure book, I went to the country for a few days, and while there, studied the volume as thoroughly as I could.

It seemed extremely difficult, and I decided to purchase another book of Troward's, in the hope that its study might not require so much of an effort. Upon inquiry I was told that a subsequent volume, *The Dore Lectures*, was much the simpler and better of the two books. When I procured it, I found that it must also be studied. It took me weeks and months to get even a vague conception of the meaning of the first chapter of *Dore*, which is entitled "Entering Into the Spirit of It." I mean by this that it took me months to enter into the spirit of what I was reading.

But in the meantime a paragraph from page 26 arrested my attention, as seeming the greatest thing I had ever read. I memorized it and endeavored with all my soul to enter into the spirit of Troward's words. The paragraph reads:

"My mind is a center of Divine operation. The Divine operation is always for expansion and fuller expression, and this means the production of something beyond what has gone before, something entirely new, not included in the past experience, though proceeding out of it by an orderly sequence or growth. Therefore, since the Divine cannot change its inherent nature, it must operate in the same manner with me; consequently, in my own special world, of which I am the center, it will move forward to produce new conditions, always in advance of any that have gone before."

It took an effort on my part to memorize this paragraph, but in the endeavor toward this end, the words seemed to carry with them a certain stimulus. Each repetition of the paragraph made it easier for me to enter into the spirit of it. The words expressed exactly what I had been seeking for. My one desire was for peace of mind. I found it comforting believe that the Divine operation in me could expand to fuller expression and produce more and more contentment—in fact, a peace mind and a degree of contentment greater than I had ever known. The paragraph further inspired me with deep interest to feel that the life-spark in me could bring into my life something entirely new. I did not wish to obliterate my past experience, but that was exactly what Troward said it would not do. The Divine operation would not exclude my past experience, but proceeding out of it would bring some new thing that would transcend anything that I had ever experienced before.

Meditation on these statements brought with it a certain joyous feeling. What a wonderful thing it would be if I could accept and sincerely believe, beyond all doubt, that this one statement of Troward's was true. Surely the Divine could not change its inherent nature, and since Divine life is operating in me, I must be Divinely inhabited, and the Divine in me must operate just as it operates upon the Universal plane. This meant that my whole world of circumstances, friends, and conditions would ultimately become a world of contentment and enjoyment of which "I am the center." This would all happen just as soon as I was able to control my mind and thereby provide a concrete center around which the Divine energies could play.

Surely it was worth trying for. If Troward had found this truth, why not I? The idea held me to my task. Later I determined to study with the man who had realized and given to the world so great a statement. It had lifted me from my state of despondency. The immediate difficulty was the need for increased finances.

CHAPTER NINE

How I Attracted to Myself 20,000 Dollars

In the laboratory of experience in which my newly revealed relation to the Divine operation was to be tested, the first problem was a financial one. My income was a stipulated one quite enough for my everyday needs, but it did not seem sufficient to enable me to go comfortably to England, where Troward lived, and remain for an indefinite period to study with so great a teacher as he must be. So before inquiring whether Troward took pupils, or whether I would be eligible in case he did, I began to use the paragraph I had memorized. Daily, in fact, almost hourly, the words were in my mind: "My mind is a center of Divine operation, and Divine operation means expansion into something better than has gone before."

From the Edinburgh Lectures I had read something about the Law of Attraction, and from the chapter on "Causes and Conditions" I had gleaned a vague idea of visualizing. So every night, before going to sleep, I made a mental picture of the desired $20,000 which seemed necessary to go and study with Troward.

Twenty imaginary $1,000 bills were counted over each night in my bedroom, and then, with the idea of more emphatically impressing my mind with the fact that this twenty thousand dollars was for the purpose of going to England and studying with Troward, I wrote out my picture, saw myself buying my steamer ticket, walking up and down the ship's deck from New York to London, and finally, saw myself accepted as Troward's pupil. This process was repeated every morning and every evening, always impressing more and more fully upon my mind Troward's memorized statement: "My mind is a center of Divine operations." I endeavored to keep this statement in the back part of my consciousness all the time, with no thought in mind of how the money might be obtained. Probably the reason why there was no thought of the avenues through which the money might reach me was because I could not possibly imagine where the $20,000 would come from. So I simply held my thought steady and let the power of attraction find its own ways and means.

One day while walking on the street, taking deep breathing exercises, the thought came:

"My mind is surely a center of Divine operation. If God fills all space, then God must be in my mind also; if I want this money to study with Troward that I may know the truth of Life, then both the money and the truth must be mine, though I am unable to feel or see the physical manifestations of either. Still," I declared, "it must be mine."

While these reflections were going on in my mind, there seemed to come up from within me the thought: "I Am all the substance there is," Then, from another channel in my brain the answer seemed to come, "Of course, that's it; everything must have its beginning in mind. The idea must contain within itself the only one and primary substance there is, and this means money as well as everything else." My mind accepted this idea, and immediately all the tension of mind and body was relaxed. There was a feeling of absolute certainty of being in touch with all the power Life has to give. All thought of money, teacher, or even my own personality, vanished in the great wave of joy which swept over my entire being. I walked on and on, with this feeling of joy steadily increasing and expanding until everything about me seemed aglow with resplendent light. Every person I passed appeared illuminated as I was. All consciousness of personality had disappeared, and in its place there came that great and almost overwhelming sense of joy and contentment.

That night when I made my picture of the twenty thousand dollars it was with an entirely changed aspect. On previous occasions, when making my mental picture, I had felt that I was waking up something within myself. This time there was no sensation of effort. I simply counted over the twenty thousand dollars. Then, in a most unexpected manner, from a source of which I had no consciousness at the time, there seemed to open a possible avenue through which the money might reach me.

At first it took great effort not to be excited. It all seemed so wonderful, so glorious, to be in touch with supply. But had not Troward cautioned his readers to keep all excitement out of their minds in the first flush of realization of union with Infinite supply, and to treat this fact as a perfectly natural result which had been reached through our demand? This was even more difficult for me than it was to hold the thought that "all the substance there is, I Am; I (idea) Am the beginning of all form, visible or invisible."

Just as soon as there appeared a circumstance which indicated the direction through which the twenty thousand dollars might come, I not only made a supreme effort to regard the indicated direction calmly as the first sprout of the seed I had sown in the absolute, but left no stone unturned to follow up that direction, thereby fulfilling my part. By so doing, one circumstance seemed naturally to lead to another, until, step by step, my desired twenty thousand dollars was secured. To keep my mind poised and free from excitement was my greatest effort.

This first concrete fruition of my study of Mental Science as expounded by Troward s book had come by a careful following of the methods he had outlined. In this connection, therefore I can offer to the reader no better gift than to quote Troward's book, *The Edinburgh Lectures*, from which may be derived a complete idea of the line of action I was endeavoring to follow. In the chapter on Causes and Conditions he says:

"To get good results we must properly understand our relation to the great impersonal power we are using. It is intelligent, and we are intelligent, and the two intelligences must co-operate." We must not fly in the face of the law expecting it to do for us what it can only do through us; and we must therefore use our intelligence with the knowledge that it is acting *as the instrument of a greater intelligence*; and because we have this knowledge we may and should cease from all anxiety as to the final result.

"In actual practice we must first form the ideal conception of our object with the definite intention of impressing it upon the Universal Mind—it is this thought that takes such thought out of the region of mere casual fancies and then affirm that our knowledge of the Law is sufficient reason for a calm expectation of a corresponding result, and that therefore all necessary conditions will come to us in due order. We can then turn to the affairs of our daily life with the calm assurance that the initial conditions are either there already or will soon come into view. If we do not at once see them, let us rest content with the knowledge that the spiritual prototype is already in existence and wait till some circumstance pointing in the desired direction begins to shop itself. It may be a very small circumstance, but it is the direction and not the magnitude which is to be taken into consideration. As soon as we see it we should regard it as the first sprouting of the seed sown in the Absolute, and do calmly, and without excitement, whatever the circumstances seem to require, and then later on we shall see that this doing will in turn lead to a further circumstance in the same direction, until we find ourselves conducted, step by step, to the accomplishment of our object. In this way the understanding of the great principle of the Law of Supply will, by repeated experiences, deliver us more and more completely out of the region of anxious thought and toilsome labor and bring us into a new world where the useful employment of all our powers, whether mental or physical, will only be an unfolding of our individuality upon the lines of its own nature, and therefore a perpetual source of health and happiness; a sufficient inducement, surely, to the careful study of the laws governing the relation on between the individual and the Universal Mind."

To my mind, then as now, this quotation outlines the core and center of the method and manner of approach necessary for coming in touch with Infinite Supply. At least it, together with the previously quoted statement, "My mind is a center of Divine operation," etc., constituted the only apparent means of attracting to myself the twenty thousand dollars. My constant endeavor to get into the spirit of these statements, and to attract to myself this needed sum, took about six weeks, at the end of which time I had in my bank the required twenty thousand dollars. This could be made into a long story, giving all the details, but the facts, as already narrated, will give you a definite idea of the magnetic condition of my mind while the twenty thousand dollars was finding its way to me.

CHAPTER TEN

How I Became the Only Personal Pupil of T. Troward, the Great Mental Scientist

As soon as the idea of studying with Troward came to me, I asked a friend to write him for me, feeling that perhaps my friend could couch my desire in better or more persuasive terms than I could employ. To all the letters written by this friend, I received not one reply. This was so discouraging that I would have completely abandoned the idea of becoming Troward's pupil, except for the experience I had had that day on the street, when my whole world was illuminated, and I remembered the promise "All things whatsoever thou wilt, believe thou hast received, and thou shalt receive."

With this experience in my mind, my passage to England was arranged, notwithstanding the fact that apparently my letters were ignored. We wrote again, however, and finally received a reply, very courteous though very positive. Troward did not take pupils; he had no time to devote to a pupil. Notwithstanding this definite decision, I declined to be discouraged, because of the memory of my experience upon the day when the light and the thought had come to me, "I Am all the Substance there is." I seemed to be able to live that experience over at will, and with it there always came a flood of courage and renewed energy. We journeyed on to London, and from there telegraphed Troward, asking for an interview. The telegram was promptly answered, setting a date when he could see us.

At this time Troward was living in Ruan Manor, a little out-of-the-way place in the Southern part of England, about twenty miles from a railway station. We could not find it on the map, and with great difficulty Cook's Touring Agency, in London, located the place for us. There was very little speculation in my mind as to what Troward would say to me in this interview. There always remained the feeling that the truth was mine; also that it would grow and expand in my consciousness until peace and contentment were outward, as well as inward, manifestations of my individual life.

We arrived at Troward's house in a terrific rainstorm, and were cordially received by Troward himself, whom I found, much to my surprise, to be more the type of a Frenchman than an Englishman, (I afterward learned that be was a descendant of the Huguenot race), a man of medium stature, with a rather large head, big nose, and eyes that fairly danced with merriment. After we had been introduced to the other members of the family and given a cup of hot tea, we were invited into the living-room, where Troward talked very freely of everything except my proposed studies. It seemed quite impossible to bring him to that subject. Just before we were leaving, however, I asked quite boldly: "Will you not reconsider your decision to take a personal pupil? I wish so much to study with you," to which he replied, with a very indifferent manner, that he did not feel he could give the time it would require for personal instruction, but that he would be glad to give me the names of two or three books which he felt would not only be interesting but instructive to me. He said he felt much flattered and pleased that I had come all the way from America to study with him, and as we walked out through the lane from his house to our automobile, his manner became less indifferent, a feeling of sympathy seemed to touch his heart, and he turned to me with the remark: "You might write to me, if so inclined, after you get to Paris, and perhaps, if I have time in the autumn, we could arrange something, though it does not seem possible now."

I lost no time in following up his very kind invitation to write. My letters were all promptly and courteously answered, but there was never a word of encouragement as to my proposed studies, Finally, about two months later, there came a letter with this question in it: "What do you suppose is the meaning of this verse in the 21st Chapter of Revelation?"

"16. And the city lieth foursquare and the length is as large as the breadth; and he measured the city with the reed, twelve thousand furlongs. The length and the breadth and the height of it are equal."

Instinctively I knew that my chance to study with Troward hung upon my giving the correct answer to that question. The definition of the verse seemed utterly beyond my reach. Naturally, answers came to my mind, but I knew intuitively that they were incorrect. I began bombarding my scholarly friends and acquaintances with the same questions. Lawyers, doctors, priests, nuns, and clergymen, all over the world, received letters from me with this question in them. Answers began to return to me, but intuition told me not one was correct. All the while I was endeavoring to find the answer for myself, but no answer came.

I memorized the verse in order that I might meditate upon it. I began a search of Paris for the books Troward had recommended to me, and after two or three days' search we crossed the River Seine to the Ile de Cite to go into some of the old bookstores there. The books were out of print, and these were the last places in which to find them. Finally we came upon a little shop which had them. The man had only one copy of each left, consequently the price was high. While remonstrating with the clerk, my eye rested upon the work of an astrologer, which I laughingly picked up and asked: "Do you think Prof.— would read my horoscope?" The clerk looked aghast at the suggestion, and responded, "Why, no, Madame, he is one of France's greatest astrologers. He does not read horoscopes."

In spite of this answer, there was a persistent impulse within me to go to the man. The friend who had accompanied me in my search for the books remonstrated with me, and tried in every way to dissuade me from going to the famous astrologer, but I insisted. When we arrived at his office, I found it somewhat embarrassing to ask him to read my horoscope. Nevertheless, there was nothing to do but put the question. Reluctantly, the Professor invited us into his paper-strewn study; reluctantly, and also impatiently he asked us to be seated. Very courteously and coldly he told me that he did not read horoscopes. His whole manner said, more clearly than words could, that he wished we would take our departure.

My friend stood up. I was at a great loss what to do next, because I felt that I was not quite ready to go. Intuition seemed to tell me there was something for me to gain there. Just what it was I was unable to define, so I paused a moment, much to my friend's displeasure and embarrassment, when one of the Professor's enormous Persian cats jumped into my lap. "Get down, Jack!" the Professor shouted. "What does it mean?" he seemed to ask himself. Then with a greater interest than he had hitherto shown in me, the Professor said with a smile:

"I have never known that cat to go to a stranger before, Madame; my cat pleads for you. I, also, now feel an interest in your horoscope, and if you will give me the data it will give me pleasure to write it out for you."

There was a great feeling of happiness in me when he made this statement, which he concluded by saying, "I do not feel that you really care for your horoscope." The truth of this statement shocked me, because I did not care about a horoscope, and could not give any reason why I was letting him do it. "However," he said, "may I call for your data next Sunday afternoon?"

On Sunday afternoon at the appointed time, the Professor arrived, and I was handing him the slip of paper with all the data of my birth, etc., when the idea came to ask the Professor the answer to the question

Troward had given me from the 16th verse of the 21st Chapter of Revelation. The thought was instantly carried into effect, and I found myself asking this man what he thought this verse meant. Without pausing to think it over, he immediately replied, "It means: the city signifies the truth, and the truth is non-invertible; every side from which you approach it is exactly the same." Intuitively and undoubtingly I recognized this answer as the true one, and my joy knew no bounds, because I felt sure that with this correct answer in my possession, Troward would accept me as his pupil in the fall.

As the great astrologer was leaving, I explained to him all about my desire to study with Troward, how I had come from New York City for that express purpose, seemingly to no avail, until the answer to this test question had been given to me by him. He was greatly interested and asked many questions about Troward, and when asked if he would please send me his bill, he smilingly replied, "Let me know if the great Troward accepts you as his pupil," and bade me good afternoon. I hastened to my room to send a telegram to Troward, giving my answer to the question from the 16th verse of the 21st Chapter of Revelation.

There was an immediate response from Troward which said: "Your answer is correct. Am beginning a course of lectures on The Great Pyramid in London. If you wish to attend them, will be pleased to have you, and afterward, if you still wish to study with me, I think it can be arranged." On receipt of this reply preparations were at once made to leave Paris for London.

I attended all the lectures, receiving much instruction from them, after which arrangements were made for my studying with Troward. Two days before leaving for Cornwall, I received the following letter from Troward clearly indicating the line of study he gave me:

> 31 Stanwick Road,
> W. Kensington, England.

Dear Mrs. Behrend:

I think I had better write you a few lines with regard to your proposed studies with me, as I should be sorry for you to be under any misapprehension and so to suffer any disappointment.

I have studied the subject now for several years, and have a general acquaintance with the leading features of most of the systems which, unfortunately, occupy attention in many circles at the present time, such as Theosophy, The Tarot, The Kabala, and the like, and I have no hesitation in saying that, to the best of my judgment, all sorts and descriptions of *so-called* occult study are in direct opposition to the real life-giving Truth, and therefore, you must not expect any teaching on such lines as these.

We hear a great deal these days about initiation; but, believe me, the more you try to become a so-called "Initiate" the further you will put yourself from living life.

I speak after many years of careful study and consideration when I say that the Bible and its Revelation of Christ is the one thing really worth studying, and that is a subject large enough in all conscience, embracing, as it does, our outward life and of everyday concerns, and also the inner springs of our life and all that we can in general terms conceive of the life in the unseen after putting off the body at death.

You have expressed a very great degree of confidence in my teaching, and if your confidence is such that you wish, as you say, to put yourself entirely under my guidance, I can only accept it as a very serious responsibility, and should have to ask you to exhibit that confidence by refusing to look into such so-called "Mysteries" as I would forbid you to look into.

I am speaking from experience; but the result will be that much of my teaching will appear to be very simple, perhaps to some extent dogmatic, and you will say you have heard much of it before.

Faith in God, Prayer and Worship, approach to the Father through Christ—all this is in a certain sense familiar to you; and all I can hope to do is perhaps to throw a little more light on these subjects, that they may become to you, not merely traditional words, but *present living facts*.

I have been thus explicit as I do not want you to have any disappointment, and also I should say that our so-called course of study will be only friendly conversations at such times as we can fit them in, either you coming to our house, or I to yours, as may be most convenient at the time.

Also, I will lend you some books which will be helpful, but they are very few, and in no sense occult.

Now, if all this falls in with your ideas, we shall, I am sure, be very glad to see you at Ruan Manor, and you will find that the residents there, though few, are very friendly and the neighborhood very pretty.

But, on the other hand, if you feel that you want some other source of learning, do not mind saying so, only you will never find any substitute for Christ.

I trust you will not mind my writing you like this, but I do not want you to come all the way down to Cornwall, and then be disappointed.

>With kindest regards,
>Yours sincerely,
>(Signed) T. Troward.

This copy of Troward's letter, to my mind, is the greatest thing I can give you.

CHAPTER ELEVEN

How to Bring the Power in Your Word Into Action

In every word you use, there is a power germ which expands and projects itself in the direction your word indicates, and ultimately develops into physical expression. For example, you wish the consciousness of joy. Repeat the word "joy" secretly, persistently and emphatically. The repetition of the word joy sets up a quality of vibration which causes the joy germ to begin to expand and project itself until your whole being is filled with joy. This is not a mere fancy, but a truth. Once you experience this power, you will daily prove to yourself that these facts have not been fabricated to fit a theory, but the theory has been built up by careful observation of facts; Everyone knows that joy comes from within. No one can give it to you. Another may give you cause for joy, but no one can be joyous for you. Joy is a state of consciousness, and consciousness is purely mental.

Troward says the "Mental faculties always work under something which stimulates them, and this stimulus may come either from without, through the external senses, or from within, by the consciousness of something not perceptible on the physical plane. The recognition of this interior source of stimulus enables you to bring into your consciousness any state you desire." Once a thing seems normal to you, it is as surely yours, through the Law of growth and attraction, as it is yours to know addition after you have learned the use of figures.

This method of repeating the word makes the word in all of its limitless meaning yours, because words are the embodiment of thoughts, and thought is creative; neither good nor bad, simply creative. This is the reason why Faith builds up and Fear destroys.

"Only believe, and all things are possible unto you."

It is Faith that gives you dominion over every adverse circumstance or condition. It is your word of Faith that sets you free not faith in any specific thing or act, but simple Faith in your best self in all ways. It is this ever-present Creative Power within the heart of the word that makes your health, your peace of mind, and your financial condition a reproduction of your most habitual thought. Try to believe and understand this, and you will find yourself Master of every adverse circumstance or condition, for you will become a Prince of Power.

CHAPTER TWELVE

How to Increase Your Faith

But you ask, "How can I speak the word of Faith when I have little or no faith?"

Every living thing has faith in something or somebody. Faith is that quality of Power which gives the Creative Energy a corresponding vitality, and the vitality in the word of Faith you use causes it to take corresponding physical form. Even intense fear is alive with faith. You fear smallpox because you *believe* it possible for you to contract it. You fear poverty and loneliness because you *believe* them possible for you. It is the Faith which understands that every creation had its birth in the womb of thought-words, that gives you dominion over all things, your lesser self included, and this feeling of faith is increased and intensified through observing what it *does*.

Your constant observation should be of your state of consciousness when you did; not when you hoped you might, but feared it was too good to be true. How did you feel that time when you simply had to bring yourself into a better frame of mind and did, or you had to have a certain thing and got it? Live these experiences over again and again—mentally—until you really feel in touch with the self which knows and does, and then the best there is, is yours.

CHAPTER THIRTEEN

*The Reward of
Increased Faith*

Your desire to be your best has expanded your faith into the faith of the Universe which knows no failure, and has brought you into conscious realization that you are not a victim of the universe, but a part of it. Consequently you are able to recognize that there is that within yourself which is able to make conscious contact with the Universal Law, and enables you to press all the particular laws of Nature, whether visible or invisible, into serving your particular demand or desire. Thereby you find yourself Master, not a slave, of any situation. Troward tells us that this Mastering is to be "accomplished by knowledge, and the only knowledge which will afford this purpose in all its measureless immensity is the knowledge of the personal element in universal spirit," and its reciprocity to our own personality. In other words, the words you think, the personality you feel yourself to be, are all reproductions in miniature of God, "or specialized universal spirit." All your word-thoughts were God word-forms before they were yours.

The words you use are the instruments—channels—through which the creative energy takes form. Naturally, this sensitive Creative Power can only reproduce in accordance with the instrument through which it passes. All disappointments and failures are the result of endeavoring to think one thing and produce another. This is just as impossible as it would be for an electric fan to be used for lighting purposes, or for water to flow through a crooked pipe in a straight line. The water must take the shape of the pipe through which it flows. Even more truly this sensitive, invisible Substance must reproduce outwardly the shape of the thought-word through which it passes.

This is the law of its Nature; therefore, it logically follows,

"As a man thinketh, so is he."

Hence, when your thought or word-form is in correspondence with the Eternal constructive and forward movement of the Universal Law, then your mind is the mirror in which the Infinite Power and Intelligence of the Universe sees itself reproduced, and your individual life becomes one of harmony.

CHAPTER FOURTEEN

How to Make Nature Respond to You

It should be steadily borne in mind that there is an Intelligence and Power in all Nature and all space, which is always creative, and infinitely sensitive and responsive. The responsiveness of its nature is two-fold: it is creative, and amenable to suggestion. Once the human understanding grasps this all-important fact, it realizes the simplicity with which the law of life supplies your every demand. All that is necessary is to realize that your mind is a center of Divine operation, and consequently contains that within itself which accepts suggestions, and expect all life to respond to your call. Then you will find suggestions which tend to the fulfillment of your desire coming to you, not only from your fellowmen, but also from the flowers, the grass, the trees, and the rocks, which will enable you to fulfill your heart's desire, if you act upon them in confidence on this physical plane. "Faith without Works is dead," but Faith *with* Works sets you absolutely free.

CHAPTER FIFTEEN

Faith With Works—What It Has Accomplished

It is said of Tyson, the great Australian Millionaire, that the suggestion to "make the desert land of Australia blossom as the rose" came to him from a modest little Australian violet while he was working as a bushman for something like three shillings a day. He used to find these friendly little violets growing in certain places in the woods, and something in the flower touched something akin to itself in the mind of Tyson. He would sit on the side of his bunk at night and wonder how flowers and vegetable life could be given an opportunity to express themselves in the desert land of Australia. No doubt he realized that it would take a long time to save enough money to put irrigating ditches in the desert lands, but his thought and feeling assured him it could be accomplished, and if it could be done, he could do it. If there was a power within himself which was able to capture the idea, then there must be a responsive power within the idea itself which could bring itself into a practical physical manifestation. He resolutely put aside all questions as to the specific ways and means which would be employed in bringing his desire into physical manifestation, and simply kept his thought centered upon the idea of making fences and seeing flowers and grass where none existed at that time.

Since the responsiveness of Reproductive Creative Power is not limited to any local condition of mind, his habitual meditation and mental picture set his ideas free to roam in an infinitude, and attract to themselves other ideas of a kindred nature.

Therefore, it was not necessary for Tyson to wait until he had saved from his three shillings a day enough money to irrigate the land, to see his ideas and desires fulfilled, for his ideas found other ideas in the financial world which were attuned in sympathy with themselves, and doors of finance were quickly opened.

All charitable institutions are maintained upon the principle of the responsiveness of life. If this were not true, no one would care to give, simply because another needed.

The law of demand and supply, cause and effect, can never be broken. Ideas attract to themselves kindred ideas. Sometimes they come from a flower, a book, or out of the invisible.

You are intent upon an idea not quite complete as to the ways and means of fulfillment, and behold along comes another idea, from no one can tell where, and finds friendly lodging with your idea; one idea attracting another, and so on until your desires are physical facts. You may feel the necessity for improvement in your finances, and wonder how this increase is to be brought about, when there seems suddenly to come from within the idea itself, the realization that everything—even money—had its birth in thought, and your thoughts turn their course. You simply hold to the statement or affirmation that the best, and all there is, is yours. Since you are able to capture ideas from the Infinite through the instrument of your intuition, you let your mind rest upon that thought, knowing full well that this very thought will respond to itself. Your inhibition of all doubt and anxiety enables the reassuring ideas to establish themselves and attract to themselves "I can" and "I will" ideas, which gradually grow into the physical form of the desire in your mind.

In the conscious uses of the Universal Power to reproduce your desires in physical form, three facts should be borne in mind:

First—All space is filled with a Creative Power.

Second—This Creative Power is amenable to suggestion.

Third—It can only work by deductive methods.

As Troward tells us, this last is an exceedingly important point, for it implies that the action of the ever-present Creative Power is in no way limited by precedent. It works according to the essence of the spirit of the principle. In other words, this Universal Power takes its creative direction from the word you give it. Once man realizes this great truth, the character with which this sensitive, reproductive power is invested becomes the most important of all his considerations. It is the unvarying law of Creative Life Principle that "As a man thinketh in his heart, so is he." If you realize the truth that the Creative Power can be to you only what you feel and think it to be, it is willing and able to meet your demands.

Troward says, "If you think your thought is Powerful, your Thought is Powerful."

"As a man thinketh in his heart, so is he" is the law of life, and the Creative Power can no more change this law than an ordinary mirror can reflect back to you a different image than the object you hold before it. "As you think, so are you" does not mean "as you tell people you think," or "as you would wish the world to believe you think." It means your innermost thoughts; that place where no one but you knows. "None can know the Father save the son," and "No one can know the son but the Father." Only the reproductive Creative Spirit of Life knows what you think until your thoughts become physical facts and manifest themselves in your body, your brain, or your affairs. Then everyone with whom you come into contact may know, because the Father, the Intelligent Creative Energy which heareth in secret your most secret thoughts, rewards you openly reproduces your thoughts in physical form. "As you think, that is what you become" should be kept in the background of your mind constantly. This is watching and praying without ceasing, and when you are not feeling quite up to par physically, pray.

CHAPTER SIXTEEN

Suggestions As to How to Pray or Ask, Believing You Have Already Received

Scientific Thinking—Positive Thought Suggestions for Practical Application

Try, through careful, positive, enthusiastic (though not strenuous) thought, to realize that the indescribable, Invisible Substance of Life fills all space; that its nature is Intelligent, Undifferentiated Substance.

Five o'clock in the morning is the best time to go into this sort of meditation.

If you will retire early every night for one month, and before falling asleep, impress firmly upon your subjective mind the affirmation: "My Father is the ruler of all the world, and is expressing His directing power through me," you will find that the substance of life takes form in your thought molds. Do not accept the above suggestion simply because it is given to you. Think it over carefully until the impression is made upon your own subconscious mind understandingly. Rise every morning, as was suggested before, at five o'clock, sit in a quiet room in a straight-back chair, and think out the affirmation of the previous evening, and you will realize and be able to put into practice your Princely Power with the realization to some extent, at least, that your mind really is a center through which all the Creative Energy and Power there is, is taking form.

Scientific Prayer—
The Principle Underlying Scientific Prayer

In prayer for a change in condition, physical, mental, or financial, for yourself or another, bear in mind that the fundamental necessity for the answer to prayer is the understanding of the scientific statement:

"Ask, believing you have already received, *And you shall receive*"

This is not as difficult as it appears on the surface, once you realize that:

Everything has, its origin in the mind, and that which you seek outwardly, you already possess.

No one can think a thought in the future.
Your thought of a thing constitutes its origin.

THEREFORE:
*The Thought Form of the Thing
is Already Yours As soon as you think it.*

Your steady recognition of this Thought Possession causes the thought to concentrate, to condense, to project itself, and to assume physical form.

To Get Rich Through Creation

The recognition or conception of new sources of wealth is the loftiest aspiration you can take into your heart, for it assumes and implies the furtherance of all noble aims.

*Items to be remembered about
Prayer for Yourself or Another*

(Remember that that which you call treatment or prayer is not, in any sense, hypnosis should never be your endeavor to take possession of the mind of another).

Remember that it should never be your intention to make yourself believe that which you know to be untrue. You are simply thinking into God or First Cause with the understanding that:

"If a thing is true at all, there is a way in which it is true throughout the universe."

Remember that the power of thought works by absolutely scientific principles. These principles are expressed in the language of the statement:

"As a man thinketh in his heart, so is he." This statement contains a world of wisdom, but man's steady recognition and careful application of the statement itself is required to bring it into practical use.

Remember that the principles involved in being as we think in our heart are elucidated and revealed by the law: "As you sow, so shall you reap."

Remember that your freedom to choose just what you will think, just what thought possession you will affirm and claim, constitutes God's gift to you.

It shows how First Cause has endowed every man with the power and ability to bring into his personal environment whatever he chooses.

Cause and Effect in reference to Getting.

If you plant an ACORN, you get an OAK.

If you sow a GRAIN OF CORN, you reap a stalk and MANY kernels of corn.

You always get the manifestation of that which you consciously or unconsciously AFFIRM and CLAIM, habitually declare and expect, or, in other words, "AS YOU SOW."

Therefore, sow the seeds of—I AM . . . I OUGHT TO DO . . . I CAN DO . . . I WILL DO.

Realize

—that because you ARE you OUGHT to do;

—that because you OUGHT to, you CAN do;

—that because you CAN do, you DO do.

The manifestation of this truth, even in a small degree, gives you the undisputable understanding that DOMINION IS YOUR CHARTER RIGHT.

You are an heir of First Cause, endowed with all the power He has.

God has given you everything. ALL is yours, and you know that all you have to do is to reach out your mental hand and take it.

This Formula may serve as a pattern to shape your own Prayer or Affirmation into God for the benefit of another or yourself.

If for another, you speak the Christian name of the person you wish to help; then dismiss their personality entirely from your consciousness.

Intensify your thought by meditating upon the fact that there is that in you which finds the way, which is the Truth and is the Life.

You are affirming this fact, believing that since you are thinking this, it is already yours. Having lifted up your feeling to the central idea of this meditation, you examine your own consciousness and see if there is aught which is unlike God. If there is any feeling of fear, worry, malice, envy, hatred, or jealousy turn back in your meditation to cleanse your thought through the affirmation that God's love and purity fills all space, including your heart and soul. Reconcile your thought with the love of God, always remembering that:

You are made in the Image and Likeness of Love.

Keep this cleansing thought in mind until you feel that you have freed your consciousness entirely of all thoughts and feelings other than:

Love and Unity with all Humanity.

Then if denials do not disturb you, deny all that is unlike your desired manifestation. This accomplished, you almost overlay your denial with the affirmative thought that You are made in the Image and Likeness of God, and already have your desire fulfilled in its first, its original thought-form.

Closing of prayer

Prayer as a method of thought is a deliberate use of the Law which gives you the power of dominion over everything which tends in any way to hamper your perfect liberty.

YOU HAVE BEEN GIVEN LIFE
THAT YOU MAY ENJOY IT
MORE AND MORE FULLY.

The steady recognition of this Truth makes you declare yourself a

PRINCE OF POWER.

You recognize, accept, and use this power as

THE CHILD OF A KING, AND HENCE
DOMINION IS YOUR BIRTHRIGHT.

Then when you feel the light of this great truth flooding your consciousness—open the flood-gates of your soul in heartfelt praise because you have the understanding that

THE CREATOR AND HIS CREATION
ARE ONE;

also that the Creator is continually creating through his creation.

Close your treatment in the happy assurance that the prayer which is fulfilled is not a form of supplication, but a steady habitual affirming that: "The Creator of all creation is operating specifically through me," therefore—

THE WORK MUST BE PERFECTLY DONE.
YOUR MIND IS A CENTER
OF DIVINE OPERATION

Hints for application and Practice

For every five minutes given to reading and study of the theories of Mental Science, spend fifteen minutes in the use and application of the knowledge acquired.

1. Spend one minute in every twenty-four hours to conscientiously thinking over the specification that must be observed in order to have your prayers answered.

2. Practice the steady recognition of desirable thought possession for two periods of fifteen minutes each every day. Not only time yourself each period to see how long you can keep a given conception before your mental vision, but also keep

a written record of the vividness with which you experience your mental image. Remember that your mental senses are just as varied and trainable as your physical ones.

3. Spend five minutes every day between 12 noon and 1 o'clock with a mental research for new sources of wealth.

CHAPTER SEVENTEEN

Things to Remember

That the greatest Mental Scientist the world has ever known (Jesus Christ, the Man) said all things are possible unto you. Also, "the things I do, you can do." Did he tell the truth?

Jesus did not claim to be more divine than you are. He declared the whole human race children of God. By birth he was no exception to this rule. The power be possessed was developed through His personal effort. He said you could do the same if you would only believe in yourself.

A great idea is valueless unless accompanied by physical action. God gives the idea; man works it out upon the physical plane.

All that is really worth while is contentment. Self-command alone can produce it.

The soul and body are one. Contentment of mind is contentment of soul, and contentment of soul means contentment of body.

If you wish health, watch your thoughts, not only of your physical being, but your thoughts about everything and everybody. With your will, keep them in line with your desire, and outwardly act in accordance with your thoughts, and you will soon realize that all power both over thoughts and conditions has been given to you.

You believe in God. Believe in yourself as the physical instrument through which God operates.

Absolute dominion is yours when you have sufficient self-mastery to conquer the negative tendency of thoughts and actions.

Ask yourself daily: "What is the purpose of the Power which put me here?"

"How can I work with the purpose for life and liberty in me?"

After having decided these questions, endeavor hourly to fulfill them. You are a law unto yourself.

If you have a tendency to overdo *anything*: eat, drink, or blame circumstances for your misfortunes, conquer that tendency with the inward conviction that *all power* is yours. Eat less, drink less, blame circumstances less, and the best there is will gradually grow in the place where the worst seemed to be.

Always remember that all is yours to use as you will. You can if you *will*; if you *will*, you do.

God the Father blesses you with all He has to give. Make good Godly use of it.

The reason for greater success when you first began your studies and demonstrations in Mental Science, was your joy and enthusiasm at the simple discovery of Power within, which was greater than you were able to put into your understanding later. With increased understanding comes increasing joy and enthusiasm, and the results will correspond.

ATTAINING YOUR DESIRES

by Letting Your Subconscious Mind Work for You

As told By
The Sage to His Pupil

The Sage: Troward Troward's philosophy as taught to his only personal pupil, Genevieve Behrend.

The Pupil: Humanity at large.

DEDICATION

"There shall never one lost good!
What was, shall live as before."
—Browning.

"I know that, whatsoever God doeth, it shall be
forever: nothing can be put to it, nor anything
taken from it. That which hath been is now; and
that which is to be hath already been; and God
requireth that which is past."
—Ecclesiastics 3: 14. 15

These pages, the outpouring of a full heart, I lay
reverently upon the memory alter of a man who
was sage and saint, teacher and guide, and my
dearly beloved friend, Judge T. Troward.

CONTENTS

FOREWORD

"All we have willed or hoped or dreamed of good,
shall exist, Not its semblance, but itself."
—BROWNING

"The thing that which hath been, it is that which shall be;
and that which is done is that which shall be done:
—ECCLESIASTES 1:9

The sages of the centuries, each one tincturing his thought with his own soul essence, have united in telling us that, "As a man thinketh in his heart, so is he." It has been established by the experience of the ages that always the law is the same. But HOW shall one thing in his heart, so that only goodness may blossom and ripen into rich deed and rare result? What is the apparently mysterious secret by which life's dull metal is transmuted into precious mintage?

It is my purpose to tell you in this little book. I desire to crystallize the heart-coinings of my revered master, Judge Thomas T. Troward, as reflected through the mirror of my mind and soul. I have adopted as my means of expression, the dialogue style, familiar to all students of that greatest of all speculative philosophers, Plato. I am convinced, through years of study of this almost superhuman mind, that this literary form is the one most nearly calculated to convey the most subtle shades of meaning, the richest depth of soul-sounding. I know that my readers will agree with me that if they will put themselves in my place, as students, and let me answer them as my master answered me, it will clarify their interest and intensify their joy in these lessons.

What I wish particularly to convey to you within these pages is the method of scientific right thinking, and to awaken in you the desire to try to use this method in order to form the habit of thinking ONLY the thoughts you wish to see crystallized in a worthy achievement or result. In addition, I want to direct your thoughts toward a better understanding of that Spirit of God, or Good, which points the way to the roseate dawn of a new civilization. The rapidity with which the ideas of man are changing causes humanity to realize that this new civilization is already manifesting itself through a clearer understanding of the relation between man and his Maker.

The epochal keynote of the present generation is that mind is the kingdom in which man reigns supreme. As the poet says, "A brute I might have been, but I would not sink I' the scale."

In endeavoring to make conscious use of thought-power, causing it to produce desired material results, mankind is beginning to understand the indispensability of absolute control.

My chief idea in sending forth this message is to make it easier for you to live in hourly consciousness that you have been given dominion over every adverse circumstance and condition which may arise. The conscious use of the creative power of thought to protect and guide you, as well as to provide for you, is only attainable through understanding the "natural relations between mental action and material conditions."

Your reading of these lessons should be with a steadfast determination to think rationally and effectively on every word, in order that the full meaning of each thought may be thoroughly grasped and comprehended. Thought-power is the kingdom of God in us, always creating results in our physical forms corresponding to our normal sustained thought. As Troward has said, "Thought is the only action of the mind. By your habitual thoughts you create corresponding external physical conditions, because you thereby create the nucleus which attracts to itself its own correspondence, in due order, until the finished work is manifested on the material plane." This is the principle upon which we shall proceed to work out a simple and rational basis of thought and action whereby we may bring into outer expression any desired goal. Let us work together to this end.

G.B. TROWARD— PHILOSOPHER AND SAGE

One of the really great minds and souls of modern times-and indeed of any time-was Thomas Troward, late Divisional Judge of the Punjab, India. Of his writings, the late William James of Harvard said, "Far and away the ablest statement of that psychology that I have ever met, beautiful in its sustained clearness of thought and style, a really classic statement." The Boston Transcript editorially stated, "The author reveals himself as easily the profoundest thinker we have ever met on this subject." The late Archdeacon Wilberforce, when writing to Troward, signed himself, "Your grateful pupil."

Responding to the many requests from Troward's friends and admirers for a more intimate glimpse of this great man, I am pleased to present to you a few phases of his daily life as I saw them while studying with him. These may be all the more interesting because of the fact that I enjoyed the unique privilege of being the only pupil to whom he ever gave personal instruction,

The Early Life of a Genius

Thomas Troward was born in Ceylon, India, in the year 1847, of English parents and Huguenot ancestors. When quite a young boy he was sent to England to be educated at Burmshtead Grammar School, but was most unhappy there, as he could not fully adapt himself to the humdrum life of the English schoolboy. Later on, when he continued his education in the beautiful Isle of Jersey, its charm entered into his blood, and he was thoroughly contended there. Perhaps the old Huguenot strain in him found a congenial element in the semi-French environment of the college. At the early age of eighteen the natural bent of his mind began to assert itself, and he won the Helford College gold medal for literature.

When his studies were completed, Troward went up to London for the Indian Civil Service examination, a very stiff one, which he passed with high credit.

He returned to India at the age of twenty-two in the capacity of Assistance Commissioner. An incident which occurred during the course of his examination foreshadowed the trend of the life that was to replace the regulation judicial career when the twenty-five years of service had expired.

"Your Head is No Common One, Young Man"

One of the subjects, left for the end of the examination, was metaphysics. Troward was quite unprepared for this, having had no time for research and no knowledge of what books to read on the subject, so he meditated upon it in the early hours of the morning, and filled in the paper with his own speculations. The examiner, on reading it, was amazed, and asked "What text-book did you use for this paper?"

"I had no text-book sir." Troward answered. "I wrote it out of my head."

"Well, then, young man," was the examiner's comment, "your head is no common one, and if I am not mistaken, we shall hear from you again."

During Troward's career in India his official work kept him very busy. His recreation was often spent with canvas, paints and brushes. He was an artist of no mean ability, especially in marine subjects, and had won several prizes at art exhibits in England. He loved to study the tomes of sacred Indian lore, or the scriptures of the Hebrews and of other ancient peoples.

While studying these profound subjects, there was unfolded to him, as in a vision, a system of philosophy which carried with it not only peace of mind, but also physical results in health and happiness.

When relieved of his burdensome official duties in the Indian Court, he returned to England, where a manuscript of some hundred folios slowly came into existence. At that time he had no knowledge of Mental Science Christian Science, New Thought, or any of the "isms" of modern thought. His views were the result of solitary medication and a deep study of the scriptures. The first edition of the now famous "Edinburgh Lectures" was published in 1904. It was received with the almost unanimous opinion that its value could not be over-estimated, as was true of his subsequent volumes. "Bible Mystery and Bible Meaning" proved especially attractive to churchmen. His books, by sheer worth, have found their way almost all over the world. In the United States alone, more than 50,000 copies have been sold. Perhaps no one was more astonished at their warm reception that their simple-hearted, fun-loving author.

An Intimate Description

In physique Judge Troward was not the usual English type, but was more like a Frenchman, of medium stature, and not over five feet six or seven inches. He was dark complexioned, with small, bright eyes, a large nose, and a broad forehead. When I knew him, he had a drooping mustache sprinkled with grey.

He had the bearing of a student and a thinker, as is indicated in his writings.

His manner was simple and natural, and he exemplified a spirit of moderation in all things. I never saw him impatient or head him express an unkind word, and with his family he was always gentle and considerate. He seemed to depend entirely upon Mrs. Troward for the household management. Only in the intimacy of his home did he entirely reveal his charming geniality and radiating friendship. His after-dinner manner was one of quiet levity and a twinkling humor. He would enter into the conversations or parlor games of the family with the spirit of a boy. He did not care for public amusements.

One evening, after an excellent dinner of soup, joint of lamb, vegetables, salad, dessert, and wine, he rolled a cigarette, and, to my great surprise, offered it to me with the Query, "Do you smoke?" Receiving a negative reply, he began to smoke it himself. Noticing my poorly concealed expression of surprise, he remarked, "Why should you be shocked at anything which you can thank God for," I can thank God for one cigarette after, possibly a second, but never a third." After he had finished his smoke, his youngest daughter, Budeia, played the violin for us. I observed that he became completely absorbed in the beautiful harmony. He told me afterwards that, although he was intensely fond of listening to music, he was in no sense a musician.

Although Troward did not indulge in outdoor sports, he loved nature, and would sit for hours by the sea with his sketch-book, or tramp the lonely moors in solitary meditation. He said there were times when he obtained his best inspirations while walking in the open. He often invited me to go with him, although frequently he seemed to be unconscious of my presence, being entirely absorbed in his own thoughts.

Truth from the Trance

At times he would lapse into a trancelike swoon (his Maltese cat on the table by his side), the swoon sometimes lasting for hours. At such times the members of his family would take particular care not to disturb him. When he emerged from these lapses of the senses, he would write down the truths which had been revealed to him. Once he wrote on his memorandum pad, "'I AM' is the word of power. It you think your thought is powerful, your thought is powerful."

It may be interesting to recall that such authorities as Barnett and the new American Encyclopedia, in their biography of Socrates, mention similar trancelike experiences of his. While serving in the Greek army,

Socrates suddenly found his feet seemingly rooted to the earth, where he remained in a trance for twenty-four hours. He awakened with a spiritual knowledge that transformed his life,and, later, the lives of many others. The similarity of the life of this Athenian philosopher to that of Troward is that both relied chiefly upon intuition and common sense for their theory and system of living.

A difference between Troward's teaching and that of Christian Science is that he does not deny the existence of a material world. On the contrary, he teaches that all physical existence is a concrete corresponding manifestation of the thought which gave it birth. One is a complement of the other.

I once asked him how one could impart to others the deep truths which he taught. "By being them," he answered. "My motto is, 'Being, and not possessing, is the great joy of living.'"

Following a Trusted Guide

Judge Troward, although modest and retiring in his habits of speech and slow to express a personal opinion, was always willing to discuss any current subject, but extremely reticent and diffident about his own writings. Never, to my knowledge, did he mention them unless approached on the subject. As a teacher, he was positive, direct, and always impersonal.

When our lesson was given indoors, he always sat in a large Morris chair, and, seeming not to be aware of my presence, he would think aloud. To follow his thought was like following a trusted guide through the most difficult places, the darkest and least explored regions of thought. As I followed, the personality of the man became obscure, and I was only conscious of the clear, commanding voice, and the light of the inward torch which he bore. It was beyond doubt quite natural that he who made so clear the true meaning of individuality should in his teaching betray little of the personal or emotional element.

After I had been carefully guided to the most comforting conclusions, in the same quiet, unassuming manner as in the beginning of our mental journey, my guide would gently remind me that he had given me a few suggestions which I might follow if I felt inclined, but which were offered only in the friendly spirit of a fellow-traveler. He always tried to impress upon me that every effort to accomplish mental control (which, in turn, meant control of circumstances) should be undertaken with absolute confidence of success.

The length of a lesson depended upon my ability to absorb what he was telling me. If he were convinced if fifteen or thirty minutes that I understood quite naturally the reason why, for example, "If a thing is true." There is a way in which it is true," that lesson was concluded. If it took me an hour or more to get into the spirit of his thought, the lesson was prolonged. At the end of a lesson he would quietly remark, "Never forget that 'seeking' has 'finding' as its correlative: 'knocking,' 'opening.'" With this reassuring statement, he would light his lantern and step into the denseness of the night to walk three miles to his home.

A Home-Loving Philosopher

Being a home-loving man, Troward delighted in his flower garden, and in the intimacy of his home, which he had provided with every comfort. He particularly enjoyed the seclusion of his studio and study, which were arranged to meet his personal needs and moods. His studio was in the most remote part of the house, and here he would spend hours of relaxation with canvas and paints. His study, however, was on the ground floor, and to it he would retire for meditation and research, usually in the early hours of the morning. He rarely worked at night.

He had spent the greater part of the day he died sketching out of doors. When he did not join his family at the dinner hour, Mrs. Troward went in search of him. She found him in his studio, fully dressed, lying on the sofa in a state of physical collapse. About an hour later he passed away. The doctor said that death was caused by hemorrhage of the brain. I am sure that Troward would have said, "I am simply passing from the limited to the unlimited." He died on May 16th, 1916, in his sixty-ninth year, on the same day that Archdeacon Wilberforce was laid at rest in Westminster Abbey. It was no ordinary link that bound these two men, as you will note in the reproduction of the letter which follows, Troward's last letter to me.

Thomas Troward regarded death very much as he would regard traveling from one country to another. He remarked to me several times, that he was interested in the life beyond and was ready to go. His only concern seemed to be the sorrow that it would cause his wife and family. When the time came, his going was exactly what he would have wished it to be.

I hope that these few intimate touches will give to Troward's friends and admirers the information they desire concerning him. I will add a more personal touch for you by presenting herein one of his first letters to me with facsimile of his handwriting.

31 Stanwick Rd.,
West Kensington, 8th Nov. 1912

Dear Mrs. Swink,

I think I had better write you a few lines with regard to your proposed studies with me as I should be sorry for you to be under any misapprehension and so to suffer any disappointment.

I have studied the subject now for several years, and have a general acquaintance with the leading features of most of the systems which unfortunately occupy attention in many circles at the present time, such as Theosophy, the Tarot, the Kabala, and the like, and I have no hesitation in saying that to the best of my judgment all sorts and descriptions of so-called occult study are in direct opposition to the real Life-giving Truth; and therefore you must not expect any teaching on such lines as these. We hear a great deal in these days about "Initiation"; but, believe me, the more you try to become a so-called "Initiate" the further you will put yourself from Living Life. I speak after many years of careful study and consideration when I say that the Bible and its Revelation of Christ is the one thing really worth studying, and that is a subject large enough in all conscience, embracing as it does our outward life of everyday concerns, and also the inner springs of our life and all that we can in general terms conceive of the life in the unseen after putting off the body at death.

You have expressed a very great degree of confidence in my teaching, and if your confidence is such that you wish, as you say, to put yourself entirely under my guidance I can only accept it as a very serious responsibility, and should have to ask you to exhibit that confidence by refusing to look into such so-called "mysteries" as I would forbid you to look into. I am speaking from experience; but the result will be that much of my teaching will appear to be very simple, perhaps to some extent dogmatic, and you will say you had heard much of it before. Faith in God, Prayer and Worship, Approach to the Father through Christ–all this is in a certain sense familiar to you; and all I can hope to do is perhaps to throw a little more light on these subjects, so that they become to you, not merely traditional words, but present living facts. I have been thus explicit, as I do not want you to have any disappointment; and also I should say that our so-called "studies" will be only friendly conversations at such times as we can fit them in, either you coming to our house or I to yours as may be most convenient at the time. Also I will lend you some books which will be helpful, but they are very few and in no sense "occult."

Now if all this falls in with your own ideas, we shall, I am sure, be very glad to see you at Ruan Minor, and you will find that the residents there, though few, are very friendly and the neighborhood is pretty. But on the other hand if you feel that you want some other sort of learning, do not mind saying so; only you will never find any substitute for Christ.

I trust you will not mind my writing to you like this, but I don't want you to come all the way down to Cornwall and then be disappointed.

With kind regards
Yours sincerely, (Signed) T. Troward

LESSON ONE

Interpreting the Word

Feeling that an explanation of some of the words employed in an unusual way in these lessons may be helpful to the student, I herein offer a list of such words, together with my interpretation and references from Troward.

Absolute

"That which is free from limit, restriction, or qualification." (Webster.) "An idea from which the elements of time and space are entirely absent." (Troward.)

Example: Thinking in the absolute would be simply dwelling upon the intrinsic qualities of love without reference to whom you love or the various forms through which love expresses itself.

Mind is absolute because of its self-reaction.

Being

Life, that unformed power of life which controls circumstances and conditions. Read Troward's *Bible Meaning and Bible Mystery*, pages 77–79.

Belief

A certain quality in the creative power of thought, which manifests on the external plane in exact correspondence to the quality of belief entertained. If you believe that your body is subject to disease, then the creative power of thought of disease results in a diseased body. Read Troward's *Edinburgh Lectures of Mental Science*, page 14.

Body

The instrument through which thoughts and feelings are expressed. The envelope of the soul.

Brain

The instrument through and in which the action of the Universal Parent Mind expresses itself in specific form as individual thoughts. Brain is not the mind, but the mind's instrument.

Christ
A State of consciousness which is altogether good, and a quality of feeling which manifests in physical form. The most perfect spiritual concept.

Circumstances
The outward effect which corresponds to the inward tendency of thought.

Conception
William James says ". . . denotes neither the mental state nor what the mental state signifies, but the relation between the two."

Concentration
"Bringing the mind into a condition of equilibrium which enables us to consciously direct the flow of spirit to a definite, recognized purpose and then carefully to guard our thoughts from inducing a flow in the opposite direction."—*Edinburgh Lectures of Mental Science.* Page 88. (Troward.)

Conditions

The result of mental tendencies. Harmonious thought produces harmonious physical and material conditions, which still further react to sweeten thought.

Consciousness

Activity of mind which enables it to distinguish itself from the physical form in which it manifests.

Create

To bring into existence. Thought is creative, because it always brings into physical or objective existence forms which correspond to itself.

Death

Absence of life. Loss of consciousness, with no capacity to regain it. Example: If a thought has been absolutely eliminated from the consciousness and cannot be recalled, it is dead to you.

Faith

"The divine promises and individual faith are correlations." Combine them, and there is no limit to what you can do through the creative power in this quality of thought.

"Essential thought. Therefore every call to have faith in God is a call to have faith in the power of your own thought about God." (Troward)

A confident expectant attitude of mind. Such a mental attitude renders your mind receptive to the creative action of the spirit of life. Have faith in the force of your own thought. You have many times experienced what it will do. Jesus' statement, "Have faith in God and nothing shall be impossible unto you." Is not a mere figure of speech; it is a scientific fact, simply stated. Your individual thought is the specialized working of the creative power of life. (All Life.)

Intelligence

The Universal Infinite Mind. The highest intelligence is that mind which understands itself as the instrument through which the Intelligence which brought it into existence operations.

Love

Universal Life and Universal Law are one.

The law of your being (your life) is that you are made in the image of God (the Creative Power which brought you into existence) because you are God's very self specialized.

The law of your life is that your mind is "the individualization of Universal Mind at the state of self-evolution in which your mind attains the capacity for reasoning from the seem to the unseen and thus penetrating behind the veil of outward appearance. So because of the reproduction of the divine creative faculty in yourself, your mental states or modes of thought are bound to externalize themselves in your body and in your circumstances." (Troward.)

Spirit

It is impossible to analyze the nature of Spirit (or Life), but we can realize that whatever else Spirit may be, it is a self-creating power which acts and reacts upon itself, reproducing itself in inconceivable forms from the cosmos to man. (Just as your mind acts and reacts upon itself when you are memorizing.) Origin of all visible things.

As it is independent of time and space, it must be pure thought, the embodiment of stored consciousness.

A self-acting and self-reacting non-physical creative power or force. Its action can only be thought because thought is the only conceivable non-physical action.

Thought
The specialized action of the original, creative Spirit or Mind.

Truth
That which lives in you is truth to you.

Visualizing
Inward or mental vision. (Visioning). Life's creating power taking particular form. The act of producing in your mind the picture of any contemplated idea.

Word
Your individual thought is the specialized word or action of the originating mind-power itself.

"That which starts the etheric vibration of life moving in a special direction," corresponding to the word, which originates special movement.

"The seed which gives rise to the thing." Plant your word-seed in the Subjective Mind of the universe, and you are sure to receive a corresponding thing, just as truly as poppy seed produces poppies.

Faith gives substance to things unseen. (The unseen word or thought.)

LESSON TWO

*How to Get
What You Want*

"Ye shall know the truth and the truth shall set you Free."
—St. John 8:32

SAGE: If a thing is true, there is a definite way in which it is true. And the truest thing in Life is that it contains inherent within itself absolute joy and liberty of mind, body, and affairs.

PUPIL: Do you mean that my understanding of Life's laws can give me the realization of perfect liberty in my individual life.

SAGE: Yes, providing you do not make the common error of judging everything from a material standpoint only. Recent research in physical science has established the fact that there is enough power in a lump of clay to destroy a city. All the average mind is able to see is the inert clay, whereas, in reality, it is the physical instrument which contains the invisible power.

PUPIL: Then when I understand the law of vibration, I can get anything I want; achieve anything I desire.

SAGE: Life fills all space, and through the understanding and use of Life's laws, you can give direction to a particular quality of creative force, which, if held in place by the will, is absolutely certain to reproduce in a corresponding physical form. What every human being wants is more liberty and more joy in life. From whatever angle you study the subject of Life, you will find that degrees of livingness and liberty are invariably manifested by varying degrees of intelligence. What you would term inanimate life represents the lower forms of intelligence; in plant life you recognize a higher degree of intelligence. To illustrate this, look at a flower. Is it not beautiful? Does it not prove to you the indisputable presence of a Great Intelligence which is expressing itself as beauty, form, and color, and above all, joy.

PUPIL: Yes.

SAGE: Still you will not find it difficult to recognize in the animal kingdom a quality of Life and Intelligence which is greatly in advance of that manifested in the flower. Then the intelligence which expresses itself in the mind of man as the power of initiative and selection is the highest expression of Intelligent Life. Thus you see that the inanimate, the plant, the animal, and the human all represent the same Universal Life, the only difference being in the varying degrees of intelligence.

For example: You are expressing a very high degree of intelligence in desiring to understand the laws of Life. When you have discovered some part of these laws, you will ascend the scale of intelligence as you make practical application of your discoveries. Another example: Two men leave college with the same degrees and situated very similarly relative to social and financial position. Both study the laws of Mind; both are obliged to struggle. One, by making a great mental effort, keeps mentally above the discouraging conditions, and finally becomes a smooth read, which the other one becomes disheartened and ill, barely eking out a miserable existence. You can readily see where the high form of intelligence was manifested in these two cases. Intelligence was there, but it could only grow by being used constructively.

How Degrees of Intelligence Prove Man's Place in the Universe

SAGE: The greater your intelligence, the more easily you can call into action the highest order of creative energy. The more highly you develop your intelligence (and I do not mean by this intellectuality or book learning-I mean self-education) the more you will find your old limited ideas of what you are not, cannot be, do, or have, imperceptibly slipping away. By using your intelligence and resting upon it to guide you Godward, you will come to recognize that you are as much a part of the very highest Intelligence as a drop of water in a part of the ocean. This steady recognition on your part, carried into your everyday affairs, will give you control over adverse circumstances, which you realize are, after all, only effects of lower degrees of intelligence, and will deliver you from falling a victim of a material universe. You are not a victim; you are a part of the Universe.

PUPIL: Just what do you mean by "effects of lower degrees of intelligence?"

SAGE: I mean, by a lower degree of intelligence, one that is unable to recognize itself as being one of the highest forms of life. The highest degree of intelligence is that form of life which is able to recognize itself as related to all existing Intelligence. For example: You can easily recall the last difficult situation you came through. It was the expression of the highest form of Intelligence which enabled you to think your way out of that.

The Intelligence Which Distinguishes Us from the Ape

SAGE: You recognized your difficulty, but you also recognized your intelligence as being able to draw to itself, from out the whole Universe, ways and means of meeting that perplexing problem. The Law is ever the same. When you are convinced that every physical circumstances or thing has its origin in corresponding activities of the mind (thought), you are able to conquer adversity in any form, because you know you can always control your thoughts. You must always be determined do to your own thinking.

PUPIL: It is not difficult for me to understand that the flower is the result of some invisible power, which must be Intelligence, but for me to realize that this same life and intelligent power in my life is not easy. I had not been taught to think in this way. However, you have made me realize that if I wish to learn, I must put into practice the directions you have given me. So when I needed to have five hundred dollars at a certain time and could not see any possible means of getting it, I tried to follow your instructions by mentally seeing myself as doing the thing I wished to do. I visualized myself paying my obligation, and in some way, which is still a mystery, I was able to feel quite calm about it. I made my mental picture and actually forgot to worry about the ways and means, and the money came. I did not quite understand then, and I do not know now, jut how it happened. All that I am able to realize is that, by my obedience to your teaching, the day was saved for me, and I shall not forget it.

Now I would like to know if we inherit our tendencies of mind

SAGE: Most of us inherit our thoughts, just as we inherit the color of our eyes. If you intend to understand the relation existing between mental action and material conditions" sufficiently well to control your circumstances, you must think for yourself, and in your own way, irrespective of that your ancestors thought, even though some of them might have brought desired results.

PUPIL: That seems as impossible as reaching the horizon. However, if you tell me that I can arrive at the place where circumstances and conditions will be under my control, through a steady and determined effort to find out the truth along these lines, I shall do my own thinking from this moment. My present condition, however, seems beyond the control of any human being. Much less myself and there have been times when I did control certain conditions, but at other times the same conditions were beyond my control. Why was that?

The Secret of Controlling Your Life Forces

SAGE: The reason you succeeded, without understanding the power which you possesses, was that you used it unconsciously, according to the law of its own nature, and reached harmonious results (as in the incident that you have just related). Your ability, at all times, to use the unfailing power which is yours depends upon your recognition of its presence. The reason for your times of failure is that the distressing condition so wholly absorbs your attention that you are unable to think of anything else. At such times you entirely lose sight of the fact that your individual mind is the instrument through and in which the very highest form of intelligence and unfailing power is endeavoring to express itself. Also, that it always takes the form of your habitual thought. Therefore, when you believe that a situation is beyond your control, so it is.

PUPIL: Which means that my control of circumstances is entirely measured by my capacity to know what the life and intelligence in me is the same Life and Intelligence which brought me into existence? The same Life in trees and all nature, and I tune in with all Life? Will this steady recognition give me direct contact wit all the power and intelligence which exists? Would simply dwelling on this thought solve any situation which might arise:

SAGE: No. "Faith without works is dead." God without expression is a nonentity. Thought without action is powerless. But your recognition that you are inseparably connected with the joy, life, intelligence, and power of the Great Whole, unwavering maintained and carried into practical application, will solve any problem, because your thought calls into specific action ideas of the very highest degree of intelligence and power, which naturally controls the lesser degrees. "The Lesser modes of life are in bondage to the law of their own being because they do not know the law."

Therefore, when you know the Laws of Life, this knowledge gives you ideas which enable you to control all adverse circumstances and conditions.

PUPIL: This is all so new to me, I do not quite grasp your meaning. Will you please give me an illustration?

How to Light the Pathway of Your Life

SAGE: Well, suppose you were in a room where every comfort had been provided for you, but the room was in total darkness, and you were unable to locate the things you desired, although you were conscious of their presence. You were told that the room was electrically lighted, and instinctively you began to grope your way along the wall, where you were accustomed to look for a light switch. For hours you passed your hands up and down the walls as far as you would reach until you were quite fatigued. You were about to give up the search and make the best of a bad situation, but, overlapping this thought, there came the resolve that you would not abandon your effort until you had located it. You were determined to enjoy the good things awaiting you, so you renewed your search with the feeling of assurance that ultimately you would find a way to turn on the light.

After more fruitless endeavor, you paused to rest, and to wonder where that switch could possibly be, "It must be here, and I shall find it," you said to yourself, and again you passed your hands over the walls, although you felt certain that you had gone over every inch that you could reach. This time your thoughts and movements were not quite so tense, although equally determined. As your hands moved slowly up and down, your mind caught the idea that the switch might not be on the wall at all. You paused a moment, and the suggestion that it might be on the floor registered in your consciousness. But reason stepped in and argued, "Impossible. Who ever head of a light switch being placed on the floor!"

"But," the suggestion persisted, "why not try? You have gone over what first seemed the most reasonable places to find it. Try the floor."

So then you began to reach out uncertainly with your feet for some projection on the floor which might be a light switch.

Finding the Light

Almost instantly your feet came into contact with an unfamiliar object. You put your hand on what seemed to be a push button, but no light appeared. Nevertheless, you now felt quite sure that you had located the switch. You paused, and involuntarily asked yourself, "How does this thing work? It won't push and it won't pull." Back came the answer within yourself like a spoken word. "Sidewise." You moved it sidewise, and the room as flooded with light. Your joy at thus finding a responsive intelligence within yourself could not be expressed in words. It was a rapture of the heart which many have felt at times.

PUPIL: Oh, I am so glad that the switch was found through clinging to the tight mental attitude! Does such persistent effort always meet with such a satisfactory reward?

SAGE: Yes, persistent, confident endeavor always brings satisfaction. In order to give you a complete picture from which you may logically reason in the future, let us consider the same situation from an opposite angle.

Imagine yourself in the same room under the same conditions. After several attempts at feeling around in the dark, you begin to feel tired, more or less discouraged, and you reason with yourself thus "Oh, what is the use? There may be a light switch in this room, and the room may contain everything I require, and again it may not." But something indefinable in yourself convinces you that not only is the light there, but so, also, are the things you enjoy and desire. You answer right back to yourself, "Well, if everything is here which I need and would enjoy, what a pity that I cannot find the switch! What a strange and unreasonable way some people have of doing things! I wonder why the light was not already turned on for me."

PUPIL: You make it seem that one almost involuntarily and invariably blames circumstances or people for his failures"

"The Fault, Dear Brutus, Lies Not in the Stars, But in Ourselves, That We are Underlings"

SAGE: You must admit that it is rare to find anyone who realizes that the cause of his failure or continued misfortune lies within himself. The reason for this is an almost universal lack of understanding on the part of the individual that a certain quality of thought brings to the consciousness a recognition of an intelligent power capable of attracting to him, and directing him so, the fulfillment of his purpose and the attainment of his desire. On the other hand, the inversion of this same power effects a negative result.

PUPIL: You mean that a certain quality of thought enables one to do and be what he wishes, while the misuse of the same power seems to thwart one's purpose?

SAGE: Yes. The idea is to use your power of thought and feeling positively, in order to attain positive results. Use it negatively, and you get negative results, because the unchangeable law is, "Intelligence always manifests in responsiveness." The whole action of the evolutionary process of Life, from its first inanimate beginning up to its manifestation in human form, is one continual intelligent response.

If you would induce yourself to recognize the presence of a Universal Intelligence which permeates all nature, you must also recognize a corresponding hidden deep down in all things-in the trees, the weeds, and flowers, in the animals, and in fact, in everything which is ever ready to spring into action when appealed to. It will respond to your call as a child would obey when bidden to come and play.

In your first experience in the dark room, your all-absorbing thought was not so much about the darkness as about the light, and how it could be turned on. The positive "I will" quality of your thought brought up from the depth of your inmost soul a steady flow of intelligent power, which finally penetrated through to your intellect and guided your hand to the switch.

PUPIL: But the second time when I also thought I must find the switch, there was no enlightened response. It seems to me that this is one's everyday experience. The first case seems like a miraculous coincidence.

Don't Look for Coincidences in Life
Every Effect Has Its Cause

SAGE: Oh, no. All is Life, and all is law and order. There are no coincidences in reality, no "happen so's." You will realize this if you will recall some of your own experiences similar to the ones used in the illustrations.

You often feel that you must have "light," and, after several attempts to avail yourself to it, your thought and feeling settle into the "I cannot do it" groove; "it may be possible for those who know how, but I don't," etc. The best method of learning the truth about this is to live your past experiences over again. Analyze what your thoughts and feelings were when you succeeded, and when you failed. Then draw your own deductions. No written or spoken words equal this kind of instruction.

Remember that all space is filled with a responsive Intelligence and Power ever ready to take any form which your sustaining thought-demand creates. This power can work only in terms of the thought instrument through which it operates.

Humanity generally admits Jesus' ability, Jesus' power to use the spirit of intelligent life to produce material conditions-as in turning water into wine, but they doubt their ability to use the same Power in themselves, in spite of Jesus' assurance, "All things are possible unto you." Now this statement is either true or false. If true it is because your mind is the instrument in and through which this intelligent Principle of Life takes initiative action, and this action, in turn, is always in accordance with the laws of life, which are subjective in their nature.

Life's Greatest Purpose is to Express Joy, Beauty, and Power

PUPIL: Am I right in concluding that this lesson in life, which is an ever-present, limitless, intelligent power, is ready at all times to be guided in any direction that my sustained thought may give it? If I permit to be anxious, discouraged, dissatisfied, I bring into action repelling, destructive forces? Life's purpose is to give expression to Its joy, beauty, and power, through Its particular instrument, my thought. Is this right?

SAGE: You have grasped the letter of the lesson in a remarkable way. Now it remains only for you to experience the happiness of what you have learned. Do this putting by your knowledge to practical application, never losing sight of the fact that no matter what justification you may think you have at the time, any feeling of discouragement, dissatisfaction, or anxiety causes the fulfillment of your right desire to recede further and further away from you. Whereas, by persistent and determined endeavor to trust your own desires and ambitions as the specific expression of the universal loving, guiding, and protecting Principle, you will find that your supply for their fulfillment will unfold to you greater and greater liberty in every direction.

PUPIL: When one does not wish to entertain negative thoughts, how can the sense of discouragement and anxiety be shut out? I am sure that it is not because one enjoys feeling worried that it seems so difficult to eliminate it. Do you mean that it is as possible to snap out of a thought one doesn't want as it is to step from one room to another? I should like to know how that is accomplished, as I have many unwelcome thoughts which I am wholly unable to dismiss at the time.

After a period they leave, but it seems to me they use their own sweet will about it. I have honestly tried to rid myself of thoughts, which seemed to cling all the tighter when I tried to throw them off. It would be wonderful to cast off a thought as one would a garment! How can it be done?

SAGE: By keeping a positive attitude of mind regarding your innermost desire as an accomplished fact, whether it be for a state of mind or for a thing. You cannot think positive and negative thoughts at the same time.

PUPIL: Oh, is that true? It seems to me I have often been speaking to someone on a certain subject while my thoughts were on an entirely different one.

You Can Actually Think of Only One Thing at a Time

SAGE: You were thinking one thing and saying another. You had only one thought. You automatically said one thing while thinking another. In short, your words were not the expression of the thought in your mind. Suppose you give yourself a test; try to think of yourself as a success and a failure at the same time. You will find it impossible to think positively and negatively simultaneously. In our next lesson we will take this up more extensively and prove why it is true. Also why you, as an individual, can control circumstances, whether they be mental, physical, or financial, through the understanding of your personal relationship to the Intelligence which governs the universe.

PUPIL: I know that what you say is true, but just what method should I employ to accomplish this? There are times when I become cross and impatient with myself because I give way to anxiety and fear (the very things which I know now will cause my defeat). And yet I will do it, just as I will eat something I like even though I know it will disagree with me. Could you give me a formula to use at such times?

How to Drive Anxiety Out of Your Mind

SAGE: When the triad of enemies-fear, anxiety, and discouragement-assails you, poisoning your mind and body, weakening your power to attract what you want, begin instantly to take deep breaths, and repeat as fast as you can, aloud or silently, the following affirmation, which is an antidote to the poison and a powerful assurance and attraction of Good.

The Life in me is inseverably connected with all the life that exists, and it is entirely devoted to my personal advancement. If you are alert and can make this affirmative thought overlap the negative, anxious suggestion, you will very soon free yourself. If the tendency to dwell on these erroneous beliefs keeps recurring, go where you can be alone, repeat your affirmation, and endeavor to lift your mind up to your words, much as you would lift your breath from the bottom to the top of your lungs. Never be impatient with yourself because you do not quite succeed in your every endeavor. It is your intention that counts, not necessarily the absolute fulfillment of the letter. The ALL-KNOWING POWER THAT IS understands and rewards accordingly. Be diligent and patient, and you will surely succeed.

LESSON THREE

How to Overcome Adverse Conditions

"There is nothing either good or bad,
but thinking makes it so."
—SHAKESPEARE

SAGE: If you wish to overcome adverse conditions or to maintain a favorable one, it is necessary to have some knowledge of the fundamental or originating Spirit, and your relation to It. The true order of these fundamental principles of life which you are endeavoring to understand does not require you to deny the reality of the existing physical world, or to call it an illusion. On the contrary, by admitting the existence of the physical, you thereby see the completion of a great invisible, creative process. This enables you to assign physical manifestations to their proper places in the creative series, which your former way of thinking did not enable you to do. You now realize that, while the origin of life is not in itself physical or material, it must throw out physical and material vehicles through which to function as its means of expression, in varying degrees of intelligence, such as the vegetable or the animal kingdom, and the human, as illustrated in our last lesson. All are forms of life, because of that inner Principle of being which sustains them. The Life Principle with which you are primarily concerned is the life of thought and feeling in yourself. You are a vehicle or distributing medium of the creative Spirit of Life. If you understand this, you will have some idea of what the originating Spirit of Life is in Itself, and your relation to It as an individual.

PUPIL: Since thought and feeling are the origin of all things, would it not be necessary to get into the spirit of their origin in order to control circumstances? Is it true that my thoughts and feelings are the same as those of the limitless Power and Intelligence of the universe?

How You Can Control Circumstances and Erroneous Conditions

SAGE: In essence they are the same. You are able to control the circumstances and conditions relative to your individual world, of which you are the center, by making your thoughts and feelings correspondent in quality (at least in a degree) to what you believe are those of the originating, intelligent forces of life.

PUPIL: Is it true that the life in me contains everything that I, as an individual, could ever require? Are my thoughts and feelings the centralizing power of my particular world? If so, then Browning explains the situation when he says, "We carry within us the wonders we seek without us." If I know and practice this great fact, the wonder of Life's understanding power will come forth in me by its own divine right, and assume command over all my problems in exactly the same degree that I recognize it. Is that correct?

SAGE: Yes, Browning has voiced the truth in that sentence. The divine Principle in you is complete, and is the only Life there is. But this should not lead you into the error of believing that you are not to exert yourself. Remember that the life-germ in you is an Intelligence which can call into specific action all of life's forces from out the entire universe, but it can only work through your intelligence in correspondence to what you confidently believe it can and will do. Therefore, be practical in your reasoning, and diligent in your deeds.

Suppose I give you an example: You have a glass of dirty water. In order to have the clear water, you would continue to pour the clean water into the glass of dirty water until every drop of the dirty water had flowed out of it, wouldn't you? The same rule applies to adverse conditions. Pour into them a steady stream of confidence in the power of God in you to change them, and they will change, correspondingly.

PUPIL: I understand. You mean that I should use my common sense, coupled with a steady faith in God and earnest, concentrated mental effort?

Common Sense and Your Mental Faculties

SAGE: That is it. Use your common sense and all your mental faculties as far as they will take you. However, you should never try to force a situation. Always allow for the Law of Growth. Remember that conditions will grow into the correlative shape of your firmly held mental attitude "under the guidance of the All Creating Wisdom." If you will follow this method of reasoning, you will soon form the habit of examining your own attitude of mind for the key to your progress and enjoyment of life. Endeavor to keep before your mind's eye the thought that every physical or material condition in your life corresponds to your habitual thought tendency, and your thought tendency will eventually become the reproduction of the way you regard your personal life, as related to all life.

PUPIL: Shall I be able to overcome one limitation after another, as I develop the knowledge and feeling of regarding the Life Principle in me as the source of all physical experience? As I advance along these lines, shall I grow into the liberty of enjoying life in my own way?

SAGE: In studying the law of your own being, the important thing to realize is that you, as an individual, are a specializing center, through which the power or essence of Life takes forms which correspond exactly to your most habitual conceptions. Try to realize more and more thoroughly, both in theory and in practice, that the relation between your individual mind and the Universal Parent Mind is one of reciprocal action. Grasp the principle of reciprocity, and you will comprehend why you fall short sometimes of enjoying life, and how you can attain to full enjoyment; just as the law of gravitation shows why iron sinks in water, and can also me made to float.

PUPIL: It is rather difficult for me to understand what you mean by the reciprocal action between my individual mind and the Universal Parent Mind. Suppose I am facing a big financial problem, and I endeavor to bring my mind into a state of confident expectancy through meditation upon the ever-present supply in all forms of life, and by repeating an affirmation which seems logical. Would tat do it? Where does the reaction come in? And how? If my happiness in life depends upon this understanding, and upon living in a state of conscious reciprocity with the Parent Mind, it seems just now that it is a long way off, because I do not grasp your meaning.

Should I feel a reaction within myself when striving for a certain state of consciousness?

How Your Mind is Related to the Universal Mind

SAGE: We said in our last lesson that your mind was at outcome of the great Universal Parent Mind which brought you into existence for the direct purpose of expressing Itself through you. The reciprocal action between your mind and the Parent Mind might be compared with a tree and its branches. Your mind is the specific expression of the Universal Mind from which it draws its power to think. Just as a branch of a tree is a specific part of a tree, not apart from it, but a part of it. Thus, between the Universal Mind or Life and its own specialized expression (which is your mind), there is a perpetual interaction, as with the tree and its parts; its branches and its leaves are continually drawing sustenance from the parent trunk. Your thought action is the specialized, identical action of the Universal Mind.

Example: Imagine yourself feeling a bit downcast, when suddenly you are handed a telegram with the news that the one person in the world whom you love the most is on his way to see you, and the messenger of some wonderful news! Can you not imagine what a definite reaction you would have from news like that! Well, you can stimulate the same quality of thought, that same feeling of joy and surety between your individual mind and its source, through mentally picturing yourself as doing the things that you enjoy. See yourself happy, and lift your mind up to it by constantly repeating a happy affirmation, and you will readily realize the reaction in kind.

PUPIL: I see. The way that adverse conditions are to be overcome is through my recognition of the reciprocal action going on continually between my mind and the One great Universal Mind, which brings about the same kind of a reaction that I would have from an agreeable experience on the physical plane. I used to think that conditions were overcome by ignoring them, and setting aside the inherent law that caused them. I begin to realize now (theoretically at least) that the laws of life cannot be ignored nor destroyed, but, on the contrary, must be made to work for us to produce a harmonious existence.

SAGE: Adverse circumstances are overcome by reversing the originating cause, which is your own thought. Anxiety and fear always attract conditions of their own kind. Reverse this tendency and entertain only those thoughts which register harmony and confident assurance, and the adverse circumstances will recede, and in their place will appear the conditions which correspond to your changed mentality.

PUPIL: Am I to regard my mind as a branch of the Universal Mind from which I draw all my substance?

SAGE: Yes. You now have a fairly good general idea of the two ultimates: the Universal and the individual, and their relation to each other. I think we should now consider the process of specialization, that is, how to make nature's laws produce a particular effect which "could not be produced under the simple generic conditions spontaneously provided by nature."

How to Remedy Nature's Shortcomings

PUPIL: How can one create conditions not provided by nature?

SAGE: Do not overlook the word "spontaneous." By consciously and intelligently arranging your thoughts in the new order, by looking within yourself for the solutions of your problems, instead of without, you will certainly find that ideas will come to you, which, if followed, will produce new conditions other than those provided by nature.

PUPIL: How can I do this? Is this brought about by causing my thoughts to correspond to those which I think the Universal Mind must have?

SAGE: Let me give you an illustration of what I mean. Take the case of a miller who has been grinding his grain by hand. His instinctive feeling is that there should be a more efficient way of grinding grain, and he meditates a good deal on what this way might be. One day, while walking in the country, his attention is attracted, for the first time, to the power in a stream of water as it rushes past him. He pauses, and reflects on how this power could be utilized for his particular purpose. "Why not harness it and make it grind my grain?" he asks himself. This unexpected inspiration thrills him through and through, not only because of its possibilities, but because of his feeling of assurance that it can be accomplished.

Immediately, the desired result begins to picture itself in his mind. By the side of the stream he sees his gristmill working under conditions, with a great wheel attached to it revolved by the force of the running water, and thus grinding his grain.

The force of the water spontaneously provided by nature has not been changed; it has been specialized to meet an individual requirement.

How Nature Working Through Mind Can Grind the Grain

PUPIL: Naturally the power of the water could not of itself have ground the grain, but through the interaction of the individualized Universal Intelligence in the miller's mind, he made this power "spontaneously provided by nature" do his bidding, just as Burbank specialized nature's laws by making cactus grow without thorns, and blackberries without seeds.

SAGE: Yes, you have grasped my meaning. Your comprehension of the interaction between the water-power, or nature, and the individualized Intelligence in the mind of man is scientifically correct. You see now that it is an entire reversal of your old conception.

Formerly, you took forms and conditions as symbols, and inferred that they were the causes of mental states and material conditions; now you are learning that the true order of the creative process is exactly the reverse, that thought and feeling are the originating causes which form corresponding external conditions. This is the foundation principle upon which you can specialize the generic law of the whole creative process, and cause it to bring all of its Intelligence and Power to bear, in meeting your particular necessity.

Showing the Silver Lining of the Cloud

PUPIL: You are right. I have been inverting the order of cause and effect. It always seemed to me that conditions both created and controlled my thoughts, that is, I involuntarily accepted the thoughts which the conditions suggested.

For example: Suppose I want to be at a certain place at a certain time. My appointment is important and I shall be late.

What a terrible thing it will be! There seems nothing to be done. That is the way I used to think.

Now, in the new order of thinking, I shall endeavor to mentally see myself as keeping my appointment, etc. I shall get into the spirit of the thought that nothing can impede my progress or thwart my purpose, and I am sure that a way will open enabling me to materialize this thought on the physical plane. I am sure that in some unforeseen way my engagement will be kept, satisfactorily to myself and to the other person. In fact, I have experienced similar episodes.

SAGE: Yes, almost everyone has had such experiences as you have related, but very few profit by them. The law is, "As a man thinks so it becomes." If you wish to withdraw from an undesirable situation, you must adopt the scientific method of affirmative thinking, and follow it up as a permanent factor in life.

You will find that the universal causative Power (call it what you will) always manifests as supreme Intelligence in the adaptation of means to ends. For instance, there is something which you wish to do-build a house, sell something, or do a kind act for someone. It is this supreme Intelligence manifested through you that guides your activities. Without it, you would be unable to outline your intention, much less accomplish your purpose. Your intelligence is the instrument through which the One Great Intelligence of the universe is constantly taking specific form. This being true, every idea which registers in your mind was first formed in this One Infinite Mind. A continual recognition of this fact will enable you to find your way out of any sense of limitation which may arise in your individual experience.

I once heard of a man who had an intense desire to do big things. He asked his teacher to think with him along the lines just discussed-that the Intelligence of the universe was taking specific form in his individual intelligence. His teacher agreed providing the student's desire was great enough to force him to arise every morning and take a two-mile walk, meanwhile meditating upon this interaction between the Universal Intelligence and its special form, his mind. The student also was instructed to form the practice of making mental pictures for the precise purpose of developing his intuition and imagination. One suggestion was that he should mentally see himself walking along a beautiful, clear, flowing river, hearing the rippling water, and seeing the reflection of the trees on its clear surface, and then to transfer his mental picture to one depicting his own desire.

After following this practice for six months, an idea of almost overwhelming magnitude came to his mind. This did not seem unnatural, however, as it was so completely in accord with his recent habit of picturing his all-absorbing desire. He joyously continued his walks, his meditation, and visualization, and finally the Universal Intelligence manifested in its specific form (his mind) by giving specific directions to bring the big idea into successful operation.

PUPIL: Could his mind have captured this big idea without the help of a teacher?

Always Lean to Do Your Own Thinking

SAGE: Certainly. The idea did not come through the teacher's mind; he simply started the student on the right track. No one can think for another. It was the result of his determined effort to recognize his own individual intelligence as the instrument in which the Greater Intelligence was constantly taking form. All that the teacher did (all that anyone could do) was to help him to hold his thought along the path he desired to go. The help of the teacher strengthened his conviction and faith in the power in himself.

PUPIL: Is this originating power of life a forming power as well as a creating and direction one, and did the teacher's thinking along the same lines steady the student's thoughts? Without the support of a more advanced mind, could anyone succeed in a great undertaking?

SAGE: Certainly. If you are sufficiently convinced of the absolute truth of your method, you do not need any sustaining force outside of your own conviction. You miss the point of your relationship to the great whole if you do not realize that it is not only an originating, but also a forming power. Do you not recognize its forming power throughout nature? You would not think of trying to make a lily a rose. If you know that the same

Power that created the flowers also made your mind for the specific purpose of operating in it, you would soon learn to trust its formative nature in its operation through your intelligence.

PUPIL: I understand. It is the power of Life in man which originates, creates, directs, and forms. In reality, there seems to be nothing whatever for man to do in this great scheme of things except to enjoy life, if he can only learn how!

God and Company, Ltd.

SAGE: The Law of Life is God and Company. You are the Company, and you cannot in any sense be an idle partner, if you wish to profit by the partnership. Your part is a big one, and there is plenty for you to do in providing a concrete center around which the universal divine energies can operate.

PUPIL: Does this mean that to realize my oneness with the joy of life I shall not find it as simple as it seems?

SAGE: No doubt there will be times when you will find it difficult to transfer your thought from externals to the interior realm of the originating principle, and to joyfully hold it there until external conditions correspond with the ideas you have in mind, but there should never be any strain. You are attracted to the Universal Mind as your source of supply, along the lines of least resistance. That is to say, along these lines which are the most natural to your individual and particular bent of mind. In this way you infuse into the Universal Mind your desires and ambitions, thus intensifying your power of attraction (relative to the desire uppermost in your mind) from the infinite forces.

For instance, let us suppose that you feel very much alone, not altogether lonely, but alone (there is a difference, you know), and yearn for congenial companionship. At a certain night and morning, go where you will not be interrupted, and mentally picture yourself walking with a companionable friend (no person whom you know, but an ideal one); then see yourself riding with this same friend, and the two of you doing many happy things together. Keep your picture in mind until all sense of aloneness has disappeared, and you feel an unmistakable sense of companionship. Let that feeling register in your consciousness, and try to recall it at will. If you will practice in this way, you will very soon realize that this is the reciprocal action between your mind and the Universal Mind. Once this recognition is well established, your ideals will begin to express themselves in form.

PUPIL: Then one's efforts should be wholly direction to the attainment of a higher degree of intelligence, rather than to the acquiring of material things.

"God Will Provide the Food, but He Will Not Cook the Dinner"

SAGE: Such a purpose is the very highest, and aspirations along this line would surely externalize corresponding things. Under no circumstances should you allow yourself to form the habit of idle dreaming. The material side of life should not be despised, for it is the outside of a corresponding inside, and has its place. The thing to guard against is the acquiring of material possessions as your ultimate aim. However, when certain external facts appear in the circle of your life, you should work with them diligently and with common sense. Remember that things are symbols, and that the thing symbolized is more important than the symbol itself. "God will provide the food, but He will not cook the dinner."

PUPIL: My part then is to cook the dinner, so to speak; to use the intelligence with which I have been endowed, by making it a power to attract, from out the universe, ideas that will provide for me in any direction that I may choose to go, according to law?

SAGE: Yes, if you choose to go with life's continual, harmonious movement, you will find that the more you use the law of harmony through progressive thinking, the more intimately acquainted you will become with the law of reciprocity. This law corresponds to the same principles which govern physical science; that is, "nature obeys you precisely in the same degree as you obey nature." This knowledge always leads to liberty.

PUPIL: How does nature obey me?

SAGE: Nature's first and greatest law is harmony. You see the results of harmonious law in the beautiful world around you. If you obey nature's suggestion, and follow the law you will be the recipient of all the benefits contained in this law of harmony that nature has to offer, such as health, strength, contentment, etc., for all of her laws bring freedom and harmony. You will find nature responding along the same lines, to the extent that your thoughts and acts are in accordance with her perfect laws.

PUPIL: Is the power of thought always creative, and does it always create conditions corresponding to itself? Can one know this law sufficiently well to cause it to respond immediately?

Fifteen Minutes Night and Day are Not Enough

SAGE: Thought as thought is always creative, either good or bad. The length of time required for the corresponding physical conditions to appear in the circle of your individual environment depends entirely upon your ability to recognize that your desired course is a normal, already existing, mental fact. It is not enough to get into the spirit of your reasoning for fifteen minutes night and morning, with the inward confidence that you are directing a certain, unfailing power toward a desired physical manifestation, and then spend the remainder of your waking moments in doubt and fear. The whole question is, how does your particular sustained thought affect you? If it stimulates your feeling of faith, the response is immediate.

PUPIL: Could you give me something to memorize which will help me to eliminate doubt and fear?

SAGE: Yes. The thought I use most frequently myself is this: "My mind is a center of divine operation. The divine operation is always for expansion and fuller expression, and this means the production of something beyond what has gone before, something entirely new, not included in past experience, though proceeding out of it by an orderly sequence of growth.

Therefore, since the divine cannot change the inherent nature, it must operate in the same manner in me: consequently, in my own special world, of which I am the center, it will move forward to produce new conditions always in advance of any that have gone before." (Dore Lectures.)

You should memorize this passage and meditate upon it, endeavoring to make your mind a "center of divine operation," by entertaining only such thoughts as you feel are reflections of God's thoughts. Whenever you sense that your way to freedom is obstructed, make a stronger endeavor to live with the spirit of your affirmation, and you will soon find your mind receiving ideas, which, if followed, will guide you into the path of absolute liberty.

The Devils of Doubt and Fear

PUPIL: Doubt and fear are the devil, are they not? Is not fear the more destructive of all wrong elements? It seems to me that it is every present in one form or another. Can this monster be entirely eliminated from one's mind?

SAGE: Surely. Although fear is the most destructive of all the mental enemies, and, as you say, seems to be ever present, yet when you realize that your fear is just as certain to materialize as is your faith, you will grow more and more guarded as to the quality of thought which you harbor. Practice makes perfect.

PUPIL: Try as I will to inhibit fear, I am unable to succeed at present. At times I utterly fail, and I am overwhelmed with it.

How to Drive Out Fear

SAGE: The moment you begin to feel fearful, get into the open if possible, walk briskly for a mile or two, taking deep breaths, and holding your chin in and chest up. Think of yourself as a monarch of all you survey and assume a corresponding commanding attitude. Repeat with every breath this affirmation: "I am breathing in the Life, the Love, and the Power of the universe RIGHT NOW!" Hold the breath a second, with the affirmation in the center of your mind; then expel the breath with the same thought and send it out to mingle with the ether of the universe. "I and my Father of Love are ONE."

If you cannot get out into the open, assume, wherever you are, the same attitude. Take deep breaths, repeat the affirmation, and you feel certain that you are protected and supplied with all the love and power which Life has to give, feat will disappear, and you can resume whatever you were doing.

LESSON FOUR

Strengthening Your Will

All we have willed or hoped or dreamed of good, shall exist;
Not its semblance, but itself; no beauty, nor good, nor power
Whose voice has gone forth, but each survives for the melodist,
When eternity affirms the conception of an hour.
—BROWNING

SAGE: The importance of the will is so frequently misunderstood that I think we will consider its true nature and purpose for a while this morning. Almost everyone is conscious that willing is not imagining. What the function of the will is, for the most part, baffles and escapes our reasoning.

PUPIL: I understand that most schools of mental science teach that one should not try to use or even understand the will, because to make conscious use of will-power leads one astray.

SAGE: It is most important that you should have sufficient knowledge of your will not to misuse it, or to be led astray through lack of understanding its place and power.

PUPIL: It is a compelling, creative power?

SAGE: Correctly speaking, the will is neither one. It is in no sense creative. There are times, however, when a strong will can compel certain external combinations.

PUPIL: If will-power can produce certain external results, why not use it to that end?

SAGE: Because I was not intended to be used in this way.

Conditions brought into existence by mere force of will lack vitality; consequently, the situations brought about by simple will power disappear as soon as the will relaxes.

PUPIL: Do the things which are forced into being through the power of a strong will disappear simply because they lack vitality, or because the compelling power relinquishes its hold.

SAGE: Both, because of the lack of any real life in them, and because the energy of the will which supports them is withdrawn.

PUPIL: I have read a great deal about the function of the will. What does it mean?

The Action or Function of the Will

SAGE: It depends upon what you have read about the different kinds of will. The will is the power-control in your mind, which holds your thought in a given direction until a result has been accomplished.

For example: Suppose you wish to go to a certain place; without the will to go there, you could not even start, not could you retain the thought of the place long enough to arrive. You would start in the right direction, and then, because there was not sustaining power in the thought, you might turn and go in another direction.

PUPIL: So it is the will which holds the thought to a given purpose until it is consummated; or keeps an idea in its place in one's mind until it is objectified in form. It might be termed a thought-stabilizer.

SAGE: Just so. It is the will which holds your mental faculties in position relative to the creative power which does the desired work. Thought is always creative, as I have explained in my book "The Edinburgh Lectures of Mental Science," page 84: "If, using the word in its widest sense, we may say that the imagination is the creative function, we may call the will the centralizing principle, its function being to keep the imagination centered in the right direction." The will has much the same place in our mental machinery that the tool-holder has in a power-lathe. To my mind this is the will.

PUPIL: It is a wonderfully clear statement. It means that success or failure is contingent upon but one thing: mental control, and the will is this controlling factor.

SAGE: The business of the will is always the same, that of keeping your mental faculties where they will do the work you intend them to do.

PUPIL: Suppose I were conducting a business, but my thoughts were more on an anticipated vacation than on my work.

Naturally my business would suffer. How could my will help me?

Practice "Will Exercises"

SAGE: The case you relate illustrates a weak will. You know that your thoughts should be kept on your business, but your will is too weak to do it. You should practice will exercises to strengthen your mental energies. These will help you to focus your attention on business or any desired activity.

PUPIL: If one concentrated his entire attention on business during business hours, would he be able to relax it later and enjoy his home and play?

SAGE: With a properly trained will, you can pick up a thought at choice, hold it until it has finished its work, let it go again, and then pick up another thought, repeating the process again and again if you choose. In short, you can work when you work and play when you play.

PUPIL: No doubt it can be done, but it seems to me now that it would be a terrible strain.

SAGE: On the contrary, the well-trained, developed will maintains any position you desire without any strain on the nervous system, and its use is never followed by a sense of fatigue.

PUPIL: I have always found it a great strain to hold on to any thought which did not abide in consciousness naturally.

SAGE: This is an indication of a weak will, which should be strengthened through exercise, the beginning of which should be "a calm, peaceful determination to retain a certain mental attitude in spite of all temptations to the contrary, knowing that by doing so, the desired result will surely appear."

PUPIL: Is the will intelligent?

"A Developed Will is the Handmaid of Intelligence"

SAGE: The developed will is the handmaid of Intelligence.

PUPIL: What do you mean by that?

SAGE: In training your will, you will become conscious of the presence of a tremendous power which acts on the plans of the very beginning, or first cause, of every so-called physical thing. This power is the primary Living Intelligence of the universe. Tell yourself what you desire in a clear, concise way, confidently knowing that it is certain to externalize itself as an objective fact, because your will acts upon the unformed creative, or primary, Intelligence, and causes it to take the form that you have determined upon.

PUPIL: That does not sound so difficult. Of one thing I am certain, that is, that my entire environment is the result of my habitual tendency of thought. Also, that when I know that I should turn my thoughts into other channels, but do not, simply letting them run along the lines of least resistance, it is because my will is weak and untrained. Will you please tell me the quickest way that this can be remedied?

You Acquire Energy, as Well as Ambition, by Exercising the Will

SAGE: I will give you a few exercises for developing the will, and from these you can fashion others to suit your own requirements. In the first place, it is important to realize that any tendency to strain will be detrimental and must be avoided. Such exercises are not only interesting, but stimulating, and if persistently practiced will keep your ambitions from lagging. They will give you new impulses, renewed energy, and determination to be and to something better and greater than anything in the past. Once you are fully conscious of the place and power of your will, in the mental realm, to keep the creative energy at work in formulating your desires, you will realize that it is very susceptible to training, and you will never again be content to live without its constant use, for it would be like living only half a life.

PUPIL: May I ask a question right here? I am a fairly good pianist but dislike to begin my practice, and, although I enjoy it once I have begun, to start is always a struggle. If I were to compel myself to practice on the piano at a certain time every day, would that develop and strengthen my will?

SAGE: It would help, but the greatest benefit would be in the direction of making you a better musician. The best way to strengthen your will is to practice exercises for the sole purpose of strengthening the will, always remembering, while taking them, that your effort is for self-training and self-control, to the end that you many realize yourself as a part of the great universal whole. In this way you gain a peaceful centralization, which, though maintained by a conscious act of the will, is the very essence of rest. With a well-developed, trained will, your thoughts will never wanted from the consciousness that "all is life, and all is good, and nature, from her clearly visible surface to her most arcane depths, is a storehouse for good."

You have the key to her great treasures, and whatever appeals to you most at any particular time and place, is that mode of the universal Living Spirit with which you are at that moment most in touch. Realizing this, you draw from out the universe streams of vital energy, which make the very act of living a joy, which radiate from you vibrations that can turn aside all injurious suggestions. This is surely a good and sufficient reason for developing the will.

Exercise for Strengthening the Will

The will is weak because of lack of exercise. Training the will is very much the same as training the muscles. Its development is gradual. Only will can develop will; consequently, you begin with what will you have, and expand and strengthen it thought its action upon itself. The weak will manifests in two phases: over-action and under-action; the former as impulsiveness, impetuousness, and the life, and the latter as lethargy, phlegmatism, etc.

It is good to begin each day with a resolution not to hurry, and not to leave any task unfinished. Effort in this direction is of inestimable value. There should be only one object in your mind with reference to your exercise—the development and strengthening of your will. At the time have no thought of your improvement as a musician, for if there is any ulterior motive, your will-training will be lost sight of.

Cultivate the Feeling of Contentment

Cultivate the sense of contentment, and begin your exercise with that feeling, determining to do it in a happy frame of mind. This is important. Take your exercise as the time of day when interruptions are least likely to occur, for seven consecutive days, ten consecutive minutes a day. If an interruption occurs during the exercise, start all over again. If you forget the exercise for one day before you have finished your course of seven days, begin the entire set again and go through with it uninterruptedly.

Place a notebook and pencil by your side before beginning. Now take fifty matches, beads, buttons, bits of paper, or any other small objects, and drop them slowly and deliberately into a box one by one, with a feeling of contentment and satisfaction, declaring with each movement, "I will to will."

The one and most important thought is that you are training your will for the particular advantage of having a trained will, and this is why you should cultivate the feeling of contentment. The only method by which you can study the development of your will is by self-analysis and introspection, so, when you have finished your practice, ask yourself such questions as these:

"What did I think about the exercise while I was doing it? Did I believe it would really cultivate my will, or did I do it just because I was told to? Did I actually concentrate on dropping the matches into the box, or was I more concerned with their arrangement, or was I distracted with other thoughts, good or bad? Was I watching the time impatiently, or was I consciously engaging in thoughts of satisfaction and contentment? Did I have a sense of strain, or did it brace me up? Do I believe that it will really train my will if I faithfully follow it up long enough to prove it?" etc., etc.

Write down this series of questions and answers in your notebook. You will find it both interesting and encouraging to keep this record and thus watch your progress.

Stimulating an Interest in Your Will Exercise

You can stimulate interest in your exercise by varying your resolution or intention. That is, one time hold a conscious attitude of joyously willing to will, another of powerfully willing to will, another of peacefully, and another contentedly, etc., etc. These variations in the exercise with the suggestions for introspection, which have been slightly changed, were taken from the best authority, as far as I know, along the lines of will-training, and I am positive will bring the attainment of a firm, strong will, and an intelligent use of it.

LESSON FIVE

Making Your Subjective Mind Work for You

"The most potent force in the universe is the influence of the subconscious mind. The proper training of the correlation between the subliminal and the objective faculties is the open sesame that unlocks the richest of all storehouses,—the faculty of remembering. And with remembering there follows natural reflections, vision, knowledge, culture, and all that tends to make of man a god, though in the germ."
—Dr. Edwin F. Bowers

PUPIL: The subject of the subjective mind greatly interests me. I am sure that had I understood what you have said concerning it, I would have realized that all that was necessary to obtain my desires was to think out exactly what I wanted, consciously place it in my subjective mind, and it would at once begin to attract ways and means for its corresponding physical or material fulfillment.

SAGE: Indeed the study of the subjective mind is an all-absorbing subject. I may be able to enlighten and help you to make working realities out of what now seems to be vague and even mysterious. But it will rest entirely with you to put vitality into these suggestions, and that can only be accomplished through using them.

PUPIL: You mean that by making practical use of your suggestions, I will be able to attain practical results which will help not only myself but others also?

SAGE: That is the idea. It has always seemed to me that the average person prefers the satisfaction of giving to another what he requires, rather than helping or teaching him how to attract the desired things to himself, which would give him in addition a feeling of assurance and liberty. You would unquestionably enjoy giving to others, and the recipient would likewise enjoy receiving, but, as a rule, it tends to pauperize the spirit of independence.

PUPIL: If I were to put into my subconscious mind a definite idea that all people have the same power in their subconscious minds to attract to themselves the things they desire through their own efforts, would that thought register in their subconscious minds.

SAGE: That would be the intelligent way of impersonally helping others to connect with their limitless supply.

PUPIL: You have told me before that there was a definite way of impressing the subconscious mind with a particular thought. Would you mind explaining this again?

"Get into the Spirit of Your Desire?

SAGE: The process is quite different from that of retaining an idea in the so-called intellectual mind. It is necessary, above all else, to get into the spirit of your desire, and an effort to feel relaxed and confident will help you to do this. "The spirit of a thing is that which is the source of its inherent movement."

For example, if you wish to impress your subconscious mind with the sense of contentment, you must meditate on the quality of contentment. See how that affects you. If in response to your meditation you feel relaxed and confident, you may be sure that your subconscious mind has been impressed with that thought.

This is getting "into the spirit" of contentment; not because of certain physical reasons, but because of your recognition of life's action in you in this specific direction. You have the whole of Universal Mind to draw from. There is no limit to the creative power of your subjective mind once you have impressed it with your intention. This example applies to everything great or small.

PUPIL: Since my subjective mind is a part of the Universal Mind, if I impress it with an idea or desire, does this impression pass automatically into the Universal Subjective Mind?

SAGE: Your subjective mind is in essence the same as the Universal Subjective Mind with which it is inseparably connected. It should be understood that your subjective mind receives its impressions from the objective mind and never from material things. It is therefore necessary to withdraw your thought from the material or physical thing you desire, and to mentally dwell upon the spiritual symbol of it, which is the inherent source of its formation.

How to Visualize and Objectify the Mental Image

All this may seem somewhat involved to you, because it is the study of the intangible rather than the tangible, but it will unfold to you as we go on, and it will seem quite simple. All we know of the invisible is gained from what we see it do on the plane of the visible. Perhaps an illustration will give you a clearer idea of that interior part of your being, which is the support of all that which must naturally subsist in the universal here and the everlasting now.

First, endeavor to realize yourself as pure spirit, the essential quality of which is good. Pure spirit is pure life, and naturally, the only thing it could desire is to manifest more and more life, without reference to the forms through which the manifestation takes place. Consequently, "the purer your intention, the more readily it is placed in your subconscious mind," which instantly passes it into the Universal Mind.

For example: If you want a house, a certain kind of a chair, a sum of money, or anything else, you should first ponder studiously on how the desired object originated. Meditating thus on the original spirit of the thing in question starts the creative power of your subjective mind (which is in touch with all the creative energy which exists) operating in that specific direction.

Suppose it is a house you desire. You will go back to the original concept of it. The idea of a house had its origin in a primary need for shelter, protection from the elements, and comfort, and out of these original desires there grew our present dwellings. So you proceed to build a house in your own consciousness first, thinking only harmonious, constructive thoughts regarding it. This kind of thinking (or building) gives your subjective mind definite material to work with, and because of its amenableness to suggestion, coupled with its native creative power, it will go ahead and eventually bring the hose into manifestation.

PUPIL: If I earnestly and righteously desire a certain kind of a home, how shall I proceed?

SAGE: You should first form a clear conception in your objective mind of the sort of a house which you desire; whether one, two, or three stories; the number and size of the rooms; how many windows and doors; in short, you should mentally picture the completed house, both inside and out. Go all around the house; look over the exterior; then go indoors and examine it carefully from cellar to garret in every detail.

Then drop the picture and well in the spiritual prototype of the house.

PUPIL: I do not fully understand what the spiritual prototype is.

SAGE: The simplest method of finding a spiritual prototype of any object is to ask yourself to what use it is to be put, what does it stand for, in other words, what is the reason for its being? As we have been saying, a house is a place of shelter, comfort, protection. It might be called a refuge.

PUPIL: Then if I want a house (really a home), and there seems to ordinary way of my having it, I am to impress my desire upon by subjective mind, by mentally picturing the type of house I want, in conjunction with the ideas of shelter, comfort, and protection, and mentally live in that state of mind, while, in order to supplement a mental atmosphere of "pure intention," I admit no thoughts of discord, such as anger, jealousy, doubt, fear, etc., but entertain thoughts of love, joy, beauty, and harmony. Would this not be literally living in my true mental abode. And could I not expect to see it objectified in a material home?

What the House Symbolizes

SAGE: Yes, because every physical or material thing is the result of an idea first possessed in consciousness. These ideas, which are universal by nature, are specialized by your mental picture, and your concentrated effort to inhibit thoughts which concern the operation of the laws of life. This habit of thought-formation, if persisted in, opens the way for the physical manifestation of the mental picture, whatever it may be, the case in point being a house. A house is an effect of a need for shelter, comfort, protection, and the life.

PUPIL: I have never thought before of what a house really symbolized. It seems quite natural now to think of it as an externalized object of an inward originating idea of comfort, shelter, and protection, which you have taught me is its prototype. Now, my natural impulse would be to go into the house and bolt the doors and windows, if I were afraid of some outside invasion and wanted to protect myself. Yes this might not always give me a feeling of security. From where does that sense of real protection come?

Living in the Sense of Protection

SAGE: The first necessity would be for you to have the house to go into, before you could bolt the doors and windows against unwelcome intrusion or impending danger. After having acquired this refuge, it alone would not insure complete protection. The feeling of protection is established within yourself through your knowledge that you are protected by the Almighty, Ever-Present, Intelligent Power of Life. Surely you know you are alive, and this understanding brings a sense of security which locked doors or barred windows cannot give.

PUPIL: It would be wonderful if one could constantly live in that thought of protection!

SAGE: It is to this end we are journeying. As we have seen, in the mind of man there is a power which enables him to contact the unlimited universal Power of God, Spirit, and thereby envelop himself in it. One of the most satisfying and comforting feelings possible is this one of being protected from within oneself.

PUPIL: I see. One should endeavor to keep the suggestion of one's real self, which is one's real protection, constantly in mind; that self which is one with all Life and all Intelligence, which not only preserves but provides for all.

To return to the subject of the house. It being, then, the outward fulfillment or manifestation of a desire or need for shelter and protection, the mode of procedure necessary to procure it would be to get into the spirit of Life's intelligent protection, and it in turn would attract the necessary conditions to bring into tangible being a house, or whatever form of refuge was most required, and visualized?

SAGE: Mentally entering into the spirit of Life's amenable creative force, it will take any special form your desire gives it, which is mentally pictured or visualized. The house is only an illustration.

PUPIL: I understand. Now suppose one wanted more money or better health. What would be the prototype for these?

SAGE: It is always best to find one's own prototype. Let us refer to the suggestions I have already given you. What does money symbolize? For what is it to be used? For myself, I find that the prototype for money is Substance, and my method for manifesting more money is to mentally picture the sum I require for a particular purpose, either in bank-notes, check, or draft, whichever seems the most natural. After making a clear, distinct picture, I enlarge my vision of money as the symbol of life's substance, as applied to the use I intend to put it to. I believe that money is the greatest factor for constructive exchange that we have today.

How to Develop Health and Harmony

In the case of money, you would hold firmly in your mind the fact that the Substance of Life fills all space. It is, indeed, the starting point of all things, whether it takes the form of desired sums of money or of something else.

For physical health you would endeavor to keep your thought as harmonious as possible, and mentally picture yourself as well and doing the useful, happy things in your daily life that a healthy person would naturally do, always understanding that the originating Life Principle in you must act harmoniously upon itself in order to produce harmonious physical results.

PUPIL: Then the most important point in demonstrating health is not so much the mental picture, as the control of thought in a definite center, irrespective of conditions or symptoms-really living in the prototype, a wholly perfect and harmonious expression of God the Father Spirit, the source of health and life.

SAGE: Exactly, and this is where your trained will comes in to help you to hold your picture and to steadfastly live in your prototype. The mental picture is the seed you plant, so to speak, and the quality of thought which you entertain most persistently impresses itself upon the subconscious mind and starts the creative energy molding itself into the form of your mental picture.

PUPIL: Then Life's only creative power is Subjective Mind, which reproduces on the outward or physical plan the idea with which it has been impressed. What a field of possibilities this stupendous fact opens up if one could only prove it!

SAGE: To obtain continuous good results it is a necessity to properly understand your relation to this great unformed, highly impressionable power you are dealing with. "Never try to make yourself believe what you know is not true." Unless your faith is built upon the solid foundation of absolute conviction, you will never be able to make practical use of it.

PUPIL: This solid foundation of conviction, how can it be established permanently? One day I feel sure of it, and the next my assurance seems to have turned to stone, and nothing I can do will bring it to life again!

Use Your Creative Power Constructively, Never Destructively

SAGE: You give your unqualified consent that you possess this creative power when you use it constructively instead of destructively. Remember, that the creative energy has only one method of operating, which is its reciprocal action from the Universal Mind to your subjective mind, and then from your subjective mind back into the Universal Subjective Mind which is its source, and which unfailingly corresponds to the thought which originally generated it. Your greatest aim should be to irrevocably convince yourself that he Originating Spirit which brought the whole world into existence is the root of your individuality. "There-fore, it is the "ever ready to continue its creative action through you." Just as soon and just as fast as you pro-vide these thought channels, you will find yourself the possessor of an unfailing reproductive power.

PUPIL: I suppose I am not unlike others, in that I am always willing to take all the credit for the good which comes to me, and unwilling to take the credit for my miseries, placing the blame on somebody or some con-dition over which I believe I have no control. How can I overcome this wretched tendency?

SAGE: I can only repeat, by endeavoring steadfastly to remember that the only creative power there is has but one way of working, which is that of reciprocal action. There is only one primary cause; the Universal Sub-jective Mind, of which your own subjective mind is a part. To gain in understanding, it is necessary to be persistent in impression your subconscious mind with the fact of its relationship to the unlimited whole. Bring your every thought and feeling into obedient connection with the best there is in you. This old saying has a world of truth in it: "What thou see'st, that thou be'st; dust if thou see'st dust; God if thou see'st God."

Hold the Thought of What You Are, to Guide You into What You Want to Be.

PUPIL: Which means, I suppose, that the law is always the same. The thought I maintain becomes a fact in my mental as well as in my physical plane, so I must hold the thought of what I really am in order to become what I would like to be?

SAGE: Yes, endeavor never to lose sight of this fact.

PUPIL: Like the illustration you gave of the house, it has its birth in the idea of protection, irrespective of any physical form?

SAGE: Protection is an inherent quality of life; consequently it fills all space, ever ready to be called into any form of expression. If you get into the spirit of that idea, you will see how quickly corresponding results will appear. Because the quality of the subject mind is the same in you as it is "throughout the universe, giving rise to the multitude of natural forms with which you are surrounded, also giving rise to yourself." It really is the supporter of your individuality.

Your individual subjective mind is your part in the great whole, as I have declared before. The realization of this will enable you to produce physical results through the power of your own thought.

PUPIL: That reveals to me your meaning in *The Edinburgh Lectures*. Page 33, where you say, "One should regard his individual subjective mind as the organ of the absolute, and his objective mind as the organ of the relative." I will never forget that fact again.

Cultivate the Idea of Protection

SAGE: The idea in the absolute is the very beginning (or nucleus) of the thing, regardless of the form through which it expresses. For instance, the pure idea of protection exists in life itself (is one of its innate qualities) and has no relation to a house or any building erected for that purpose.

PUPIL: Then it is my objective mind or intellect which suggests to this self-existing, absolute power the idea of this relationship?

SAGE: Quite so, and if you will pattern the thought you have just expressed, telling your subconscious mind over and over again that it is the one and only creative power, which always brings into physical manifestation corresponding forms of the ideas with which it is impressed, you will realize the joys of success.

PUPIL: I "see through a glass darkly." Is there no way to develop a keener sense of just how to awaken the subconscious mind so that it will respond more quickly?

SAGE: I will be happy to give you a copy of a letter I once wrote in response to a question similar to yours. This letter was considered so helpful that the men to whom it was written had it put into pamphlet form, now out of print. It seems to me that the main thing that I said in that letter was "Don't try!"

PUPIL: Why! I thought that trying was to be my main endeavor, even though it was difficult?

A Letter of Golden Leaves
The Sage's Letter

To answer your question as to how a "Keener sense of the subjective mind may be awakened," the answer is "Don't try. Don't try to make thing what they are not." Subjective mind is subjective just because it lies below the threshold of consciousness. It is the Builder of the Body, but we can neither see, hear, nor feel it building.

Just keep in your conscious mind a quiet, calm expectation that subjective mind is always at work in accordance with the habitual thought of your objective mind . . . and then subjective mind will take care of itself.

Then the question is, how to keep the conscious thought in a life-enjoying and life-giving current. My answer to this is very simple, thought perhaps old-fashioned. It is, keep looking at God. Don't trouble about theology, but try to realize the Universal Divine Spirit as perpetually flowing through all things; through insensible things as atomic energy; through animals as instinct; through man as thought.

If this be so, then your manifestation of God will correspond with your habitual thought of God. Quietly contemplate the Divine Spirit as a continual flowing of Life, Light, Intelligence, Love and Power, and you will find this current flowing through you and manifesting in a hundred ways, both mentally and physically, in your affairs.

You do not make this current, but you prepare the conditions which will either cause it to trickle through thinly and weakly, or flow through strongly. You prepare the conditions on the interior side by a mental attitude of looking into the light (God is Light) with the expectancy of thence receiving life and Illumination, and on the exterior side by not denying in your work what you are trying to hold in your thought, -for yourself the simple Law of Enjoyment of all that you can enjoy, ruled by moderation, and toward others equally simple Law of Honesty and Kindness.

I know you have heard these things ever since you were a child, but what we all want is to realize our connection with the building power within. The connection is this: that the Spirit, as it flows through you, becomes you, and it becomes in you just what you take it fork, just as water takes the shape of the pipe it flows through. It takes shape from your thought. It is exceedingly sensitive-how much more, then, must the pure Life Principle itself be sensitive? Think over this. Think it over and then think. Think of it kindly, lovingly, trustfully, and as a welcome companion. It will respond exactly. Think of it as a Living Light, continually flowing through and vivifying you, and it will respond exactly.

If you ask why it does this, the answer is because IT is the Infinite of your Real Self. Let this answer suffice you. You will only darken the Light by trying to analyze the Divine Spirit. You cannot dissect God. This doesn't mean being impractical, but getting to the very root of truly practical. We have our ordinary business to do, but, believe me, it is the scientific method to bring everything into the Divine Light.

Then let your ideas be desires to see it in the Divine Light, let your ideas regarding it grow quietly of themselves, and you will see it in its proper and true light whatever the thing may be.

Then when you have seen what the thing really is, go on and handle it in accordance with the four principles of Cheerfulness, Moderation, Honestly and Kindness. Don't worry, and don't try to force things; let them grow, because, by recognizing the continual flow of the Spirit, you are providing the conditions, for Life is the Light which will make them grow the right way.

Don't bother about subjective mind and objective mind, or theories of any sort, or description, either mine or anyone else's; but just do what I have said and try it for six months, and I think you will find you have got hold of the Power that Works, and, after all, that is what we want.

It is all summed up in this: Live naturally with the Spirit and don't worry. Remember, you and your Spirit are One, and it is all quite natural. You will perhaps say that this is too simple. Well, we don't want to introduce unnecessary complications. Try practicing and leave the theory to take care of itself. Living Spirit is not to be found in a book."

SAGE: Many have written me from all parts of the world voicing you expression. Once a lady in New York City wrote asking me to explain to her exactly what I mean in the pamphlet about Spirit becoming you. Thinking you might like to see a copy of my reply, I brought it along for you.

PUPIL: Thank you so much. Am I at liberty to keep these letters?

SAGE: Quite.

The Letter of the Master

With regard to the sentence in the pamphlet on the Subjective Mind about the Spirit becoming you, I really don't see how to express my meaning any more clearly. What I mean is that in a cat it becomes a cat; and in a cabbage it becomes a cabbage; but in man, who is conscious, living intelligence, it becomes conscious, living intelligence. And if so, then since the Spirit is Infinite you can by prayer and meditation draw upon it for increase living intelligence, i.e., all depends on your mode of recognition of it.

In the sentence you quote, "It is exceedingly sensitive," etc,. I am not referring to the water, but the Spirit. I mean that if subconscious mind in ourselves is sensitive to suggestion, the creative principle is sensitive to suggestion, the creative principle from which it springs must be still more so, and takes shape from your thought accordingly. But you must remember that the pamphlet was not written for publication. It was merely a private letter, and I was never consulted on the subject of publishing it, or perhaps I should have worded it more carefully.

Supply and demand is a very large subject, but eventually you will always have to come back to the teaching of Jesus, "Ask and ye shall receive." We may write volumes on the subject, but in the end it always comes to this, and we have gained nothing by going a long way around. I am coming more and more to see that the teaching of Jesus is the final embodiment of all that writers on those subjects are trying to teach. In the end we have to drop all our paraphernalia of argument and come back to His statement of the working method. All the Bible premises are based on the divine knowledge of your mental constitution, and by simple reliance on it we therefore afford centers through which the Creative Power of the Universe can act in correspondence with our recognition of it. "According to your faith so be it unto you." Our faith is our real thought. If our real thought is expectation of disease and poverty, and so open the door to it. The whole purpose of the Bible is to direct our thought (which is our faith) in the right way, instead of leaving us to form it invertedly. Therefore, as the basis for our faith, the Bible gives us Promises. Pin your faith to the Promises, and you need not bother your brains to argue about it. The more you argue, the more you will pin your faith to your own argument and your understanding of the law; and as a logical sequence you make the fulfillment of your desire depend on your correct arguing and exact knowledge, so that the result is you are depending entirely upon yourself, and so you are "no forarder" and are just simply where you were.

On the other hand by simply believing the Divine Promises, you transfer the whole operation to the Divine Spirit (your subjective mind), and so you have a good ground of expectation, and by your mental receptive attitude you become a "fellow worker" with God. You allow the All Creating Spirit to work in, for, and through you. This is the conception of St. Paul always had in his epistles, in all of them showing the weakness of relying on Law, and the strength of Faith in Promises. This also, I think, was Jesus' meaning when He said: "'Blessed is he that hath not seen and yet hath believed." Well, I hope that these few remarks will be useful to you, but I am wondering how this point of view will appeal to an American audience, and that is another reason why I am rather doubtful about coming over. The more I think of this subject, the less I see in trying to make "Supply," "Health," and all the usual New Thought topics the subject of a set of mechanical rules like the rules of arithmetic. It throws the burden back on yourself, while your whole object is to get rid of it. It is the old temptation of Eden over again-the Tree of Knowledge, reliance on our own acquisition of Knowledge; on the Tree of Life—reliance of God's own nature and His desire for expression in us and through us, which is the meaning of all the promises. The former looks clever but isn't.

The latter looks childish but is the fulfillment of all law, and is life.

If you see things in this light, which I am sure is the true one, the model you will have to take for the "School of the Builders" is "The stone which the builders rejected has become the head of the corner." The reference is to the great pyramid and the topmost stone—also to our crowning stone in Westminster Abbey—and of course it refers superlatively to Christ. But properly instructed builders do not reject this stone. On the contrary, they recognize it as both the Foundation and the apex of the Building of the Temple. You remember how St. Paul calls himself a wise master-builder. Is it any use for me to come to America to teach these things, which is some form or another have been taught there ever since the arrival of the Mayflower? Of course, I can talk about Vibration, Nervous System, the Pyramid, and the like, and the working of Natural Laws; but the Creating Principle is apart.

A worshipper of God and a student of Nature, is what one of our old thinkers called himself. The Power is of God and is received by Man and Man exercises it upon nature. That is the true order.

One meaning of the Masonic symbol of the five pointed star is that everything returns to its starting point. Start from the apex of the triangle and trace the line around and you come back to the apex. If, then, your starting point is in Heaven, you go back to Heaven and the Divine Power, and so get rid of the burden; but if your starting point is on earth (i.e., your own acquisition of knowledge of laws), you get back to earth, which is indicated by the inverted triangle.

You will find the Promises of man's power over Nature, Conditions, etc., fully stated in Mark 11: 22–25, and no teaching can promise more than this.

God Has Ripened a Great Mind

PUPIL: No words can express what a privilege I feel it to have you thus unfold and make clear to me the truths I have struggled so hard to understand. God has surely blessed you with one of the greatest minds of the present generation.

SAGE: Not at all. There are many who know much more than I along these lines. For myself, however, I am certain that there is but one God, that God and man are one, and that my mind is a center of Divine Operation; this in itself is a blessing.

Much has already been written on these subjects; it is all so simple.

PUPIL: I know it is simple to you, but to us, who are struggling between certainty and uncertainty, it is a rare benefit to be able to sit and listen at the feet of certainty.

SAGE: I am happy indeed that these lessons have been helpful. It has been a great pleasure for me to have exchanged ideas with you, and I know that you will pass them on to others whenever you feel they will be helpful. It seems to me that you now have all the material necessary to build for yourself a foundation and superstructure of absolute faith in God and of the power of God in you, which is your subjective mind. This knowledge, well established, gives you dominion over every adverse circumstance and condition, because you are in conscious touch with your limitless supply. "Only believe in the God within, and all things are possible unto you."

LESSON SIX

Hourly Helps

SAGE: I want in this lesson to give you, in the most practical form, the means whereby you may meet the disquieting things of life-the things which wear soul, spirit, and body almost to the snapping point. I want you to take these admonitions and instructions into your most intimate life and keep them bright and shining by daily use. They will help you hourly in overcoming destructive elements, and in attracting constrictive ones.

Anger

When anger begins to stir you, take deep breaths; hold your thought on the inflow of breath as being rays of light, breathing deeper and deeper. Continue the deep breaths until you have taken twenty-five inhalations; hold each one while you count to seven. Then expel slowly, keeping your thought steadily on the inhalation, mentally seeing it go all through your lungs, and penetrating every part of your body s rays of light. Then meditate upon any real live thought about yourself, such as being one with all life and good. A little practice in this way will soon relieve you of the tendency to anger.

Anxiety

When conditions are not to your liking and you find yourself thinking more and more about how unhappy you are because of them, stay out of doors in the open all you possibly an.

Endeavor to walk at least two miles every day, breathing deeply of the fresh air with this thought: "I am breathing in the Life, the Love and the Power of the universe, right now." Do not permit your thought to slip back into the old groove. Fill your mind with this declaration about yourself. You have been given dominion over every adverse condition through your power of thought. Persist in your steady recognition of this fact. Tell yourself over and over again that all is well right now in your thought and feeling' consequently outside conditions must and will correspond.

Disease

If your body is the expression of thought, then disease must be the result of a belief that your body is subject to disease. Tell yourself many times a day that all physical disease is the result of discordant thoughts, and when you have actually accepted this statement as a truth, you will be careful to entertain only healthy, harmonious thoughts for yourself or another. For example, if you feel a headache coming on, begin at once to take deep breaths, and repeat with each breath that breath is Life, and that life is perfect health. "I am alive, so the health of life is manifesting in me right now."

Disappointment

This subtle destructive power should be shut out at all times by the recognition of your direct contact with all the joy there is, because you are one with its Source, Universal Good. If the joyous life does not express itself through the exact channels which you expect, know that it will do so through others. Life wants to express joy through you, for it made you an instrument in which and through which to do it. Because you are here for that purpose. You can and do enjoy all the good which Life has to give. Take some physical exercises while holding that thought. A good one is to sit on a chair and take a deep breath; then slowly exhale, and as you exhale, gradually bend at the hips until you can touch the floor with the tips of your fingers. Repeat this seven times with the affirmation: "The joy of God is flowing in me and through me right now."

Discontent

When this enemy to peace and happiness begins to advance, sing, sing sing, right out loud if you can, or else do it mentally. Sing anything you like. Watch your breath control, and every night put into your subconscious mind the thought that God brought you into existence for the purpose of expressing all of Life's harmonies, both in you and through you, and it is your divine right to BE harmony and to be harmonious in your daily experience. Meditate upon the harmony you see expressed in nature and endeavor to apply it in your thought, and then express it.

Discouragement

This is failure on your part to recognize the Almighty limitless Source of Supply (God) as your never-failing, co-operative partner. When you are assailed with the thought of discouragement, immediately ask yourself, "What kind of a power was it that brought me into existence, and for what purpose?" Then repeat slowly and thinkingly, "I do believe and I am persuaded that

God is an ever-present, never-failing source of protection and supply." Watch your thoughts lest any contrary to this affirmation be lurking around in the corners of your mind, and stick to it with all the will that you have, and you will break down the suggestion that there is any power in discouragement.

Envy

Envy is due to a sense of separation from God, Good. Endeavor to realize that where there is life, all that life has to give is present in its entirety at all times and in all places, and will come into visible expression through the persistent recognition of this grand fact.

Fear

One writer has said that fear is the only devil there is. Certainly it is the most destructive power one can entertain. When fear comes to assail you, close the door of your mind against it with this positive thought: "The only creative power there is, is thought. All things are possible to him who believes that the God which brought man into existence did so for the purpose of expressing His Fatherly love and protection in His child. I believe in God, the Father almighty, as my life, my intelligence, manifesting in my consciousness now." As you think this, walk briskly or take strenuous exercise. Whenever you sense fear returning, inhibit it instantly by substituting any thought which affirms the power of God in you. In short, fear is absolutely overcome by withdrawing your thought from the physical reason or argument which would cause you to believe in a power other than God, and the spirit of Life and Love as your birthright.

Indecision

This is a lack of the realization that your intelligence is the instrument through which the Intelligence of the universe takes specific form. An effort to realize this fact should be a habit of mind, rather than spasmodic attempts made only with the necessity for decision arises.

Jealousy

This is love's greatest enemy, and if permitted to dwell within your consciousness, will ultimately destroy your ability to enjoy your life. It is the reaction of the fear of loss and can be overcome through prayer and watchfulness. Reason along these lines: "God is Life and God is Love. I am life and I am love. I cannot lose Love any more than I can lose Life." When you are tempted to feel jealous, walk long distances as frequently as possible and keep your thought on Love itself, not on any one person whom you love, but just Love and its attributes. Think of God as Love. Keep all thought of personality out of mind, and you will find that love will spring up in you as a fountain of everlasting love and life and fill your consciousness through and through.

Self-Condemnation

The instant you begin to blame yourself to having done the wrong thing or for not having done the right thing, put this thought into your consciousness to the exclusion of every other: "Infinite Intelligence and Wisdom are expressing themselves in me more and more right now." Take the exercise of bending the body from the hips (without bending the knees) so that you can touch the floor with the tips of your fingers, inhaling as you lift the body, and exhaling every time you bend. Repeat this exercise sixteen times, accompanied by the affirmation just given.

Self-Indulgence

This is brought about by lack of will-power: an evidence of a weak will. It means failure, because you have no thought-power to give the unformed energy f life the particular thought-material necessary to produce desired results.

Absolute mental (thought) control is the one and only thing which is necessary for you to do, to be, or to have what you want. Without it, you scatter your forces.

If you permit your thoughts to run riot without restraint, the conditions of your life will become chaotic. For example: A friend does something of which you do not approve, or perhaps your present circumstances are undesirable.

Refuse to let your thought dwell on the injustice of your friend, for dwelling on it would only produce greater unhappiness for you. Control your thought and do not think of your friend in this connection. Instead, consider the many fine attributes of friendship, and this will restore harmony. Do the same in regard to your unpleasant circumstances. Don't picture them mentally and say to yourself, "How dreadful they are!" But repeat the glorious truth which I have previously referred to: "My mind is a center of divine operation." etc., and divine operation is always for greater advancement and better things. You will experience this if you cling faithfully to this line of reasoning.

Sensitiveness

A highly sensitive mind is simply a "self-mind," a form of unadulterated selfishness. Your feelings are hurt because someone says something which you do not life, or dos something which displeases you. Or conversely, he fails to say or to do what you think he should. To eradicate this baneful though-habit, use the same method of argument as for self-indulgence, and if faithful in your mental work, your efforts will be rewarded, and you will free yourself.

Unhappiness

A continually unhappy state of mind is the direct result of constantly viewing life from the physical standpoint as though that were life's only reality. Every night, before you go to sleep, put well into your subconscious mind this thought: "There is but One Mind to think about me or to make laws over me, and that is the Mind of Divine Love and Divine Power." Every morning meditate upon this thought. Use it as your shield and buckler at the first suggestion of any sense of unhappiness. You will soon find that the tendency to be discontented and unhappy will vanish, and happier conditions will come into your experience.

LESSON SEVEN

Putting Your Lessons into Practice

Just as I am completing this manuscript for the printer, the idea suggests itself that it will also be helpful to give a definite idea, in formula form, of how to be and have what you want.

First, you should endeavor to learn to be as near the perfect reflection of your own idea of God as possible, in thought and action. It may seem impossible at first thought, to even approach such a goal, but reflection upon the thought that God made you out of Himself, because He wised to see and feel Himself in you, will help you to persevere. When you first began to learn to read, no doubt you felt in your childish way that it would be wonderful to read as well as the grown-ups could; you kept on trying and then you read.

Perhaps you have a big desire which you would give your life to have fulfilled. In reality it is only necessary for you to give a few moments each day to earnest effort, in getting into the spirit of this idea of God and living in it every waking hour. Then endeavor to find the Spiritual Prototype for your desire. By this I mean inhibit all thought of the physical side of your desire.

If you desire a true companion, close your mind entirely to all personality and physical being, and dwell in thought and feeling on the spirit of love and true comradeship, without reference to any physical person. The person is the instrument through which these particular qualities manifest, and not the qualities themselves, as we often learn too late.

Or you may desire improved financial condition. Here again it is not mere money you desire. It is that which money symbolizes—Substance, Liberty, Freedom from lack.

Therefore, you should go alone night and morning (or any time when you are certain you will not be disturbed) and meditate first upon your own true relation to God. After your feeling has been stimulated to the point of certainty, then meditate upon the ever-present, never-failing substance and freedom of God. Try not to lose sight of the fact that the greatest magnet for acquiring money is Ideas. There is every reason that you should capture one of these big money ideas, if you will persistently follow the suggestions given.

If you do this, you will not only capture the idea, but also the courage to put the idea into practical application. This courage, put to positive uses, will bring you to the goal of your desire—substance, love, friends, health, happiness, and the peace that passeth all understanding.

May all these come to you in richest measure.

AFTERWORD

I love Genevieve Behrend.

In a time when many women were "invisible" in the world due to male dominated living, Genevieve was learning and sharing. This 1921 book became her most famous work, though she wrote others.

One of the reasons for its success is her ability to take complicated subjects and express them in simple terms. She made creating your own reality through imagery and belief a doable thing. Just follow her clear instructions and you too can be living a far more abundant life.

She did far more than write three books. She founded a school in New York, gave lectures, and brought the message of Mental Science to the masses.

She later founded another school in Los Angeles. She taught for about 35 years.

Her work influenced me, too. I found a rare copy of her book, *Attaining Your Desires*, and republished it. I loved how she explained how to create my reality by visualizing what I wanted. She taught me how to operate my subconscious mind, and the results were spectacular.

What you just read is pure gold. I urge you to reread it and apply it. This is the stuff of giants, and the way to magic and miracles.

Dr. Joe Vitale
www.MrFire.com.

ABOUT THE AUTHOR

Genevieve Behrend (1881 in Paris–1960 in United States) was a French-born author and teacher of Mental Science, a New Thought discipline created by Thomas Troward.

There is little known about her early life except that one of her parents was Scottish. After her husband died she traveled extensively. She studied Christian Science and met its founder Mary Baker Eddy, but ultimately left that faith. She met Abdul Baha, whose father had founded Bahá'í Faith, and he told her that she would "travel the world over seeking the truth, and when [she] had found it, would speak it out." She later wrote that she found a book of Thomas Troward's lectures. Inspired by this, she wanted to study with Troward (who was known as the master of Mental Science), but lacked the money to travel to Cornwall, England where he lived, as she was then living in New York. So every night and morning she visualized counting out twenty $1,000 bills, buying her ticket to London, traveling on the ship, and being accepted as Troward's pupil. She also constantly affirmed to herself, "My mind is a center of Divine operations." Then, to quote her in *Your Invisible Power*:

> *"While these reflections were going on in my mind, there seemed to come up from within me the thought: 'I am all the substance there is.' Then, from another channel in my brain the answer seemed to come, 'Of course, that's it; everything must have its beginning in mind. The 'I', the Idea, must be the only one and primary substance there is, and this means money as well as everything else.' My mind accepted this idea, and immediately all the tension of mind and body was relaxed."*

In about six weeks, she received the money. From 1912 to 1914, her life focused solely on the wisdom and philosophy of Troward whose influential and compelling ideas provided much of the groundwork to the spiritual philosophy known today as New Thought. As the awareness of "mental science" was taking shape, Troward imparted his personal insight to only one pupil who could perpetuate this knowledge and share it with the world. Behrend was the only personal student Troward had throughout his life.

After her studies with Troward, around 1915, she founded a New Thought school called The School of the Builders in New York City, running it herself until 1925. She then established another school in Los Angeles before touring other major cities throughout North America for the next 35 years as a celebrated lecturer, teacher, and practitioner of "Mental Science." She is quoted as an expert in the best-selling self-help book *The Secret* by Rhonda Byrne.

Millions heard and enjoyed her, not only on the public platform but over the radio. Her students numbered tens of thousands all over the English-speaking world. *Your Invisible Power* was her first book and remains her most powerful and popular work, and, since its first edition, one of the world's best sellers on Mental Science. It has exhausted scores of editions.

Behrend presents the Troward philosophy at its best because of the way her incomparably direct, and dynamic personality relates the life-changing concepts on a personal level.

This book can teach you how to use the power of visualization and other processes taught by Thomas Troward to transform your life. *Your Invisible Power* is a powerful, yet simple and easy guide.

Behrend says, "We all possess more power and greater possibilities than we realize, and visualizing is one of the greatest of these powers. It brings other possibilities to our observation. When we pause to think for a moment, we realize that for a cosmos to exist at all, it must be the outcome of a cosmic mind. These pages have been written with the purpose and hope that their suggestions may furnish you a key to open up the way to the attainment of your desires."

This book can teach you how to use the power of visualization and other processes taught by Thomas Troward to transform your life.